# THE
*TOWN & COUNTRY*
# WORLD
# OF GOLF

# THE
# TOWN & COUNTRY
# WORLD
## —OF—
# GOLF

## RICHARD MILLER

TAYLOR PUBLISHING COMPANY
DALLAS, TEXAS

*To all my wonderful friends*

Published by Taylor Publishing Company
             1550 West Mockingbird Lane
             Dallas, Texas 75235

Designed by Walter Gray Lamb

**Library of Congress Cataloging-in-Publication Data**

Miller, Dick, 1936-
    Town & country's world of golf / Richard Miller.
        p.   cm.
    ISBN 0-87833-805-5
        1.  Golf—United States.   2.  Golf courses—United States.
    I.  Town & country.   II. Title.   III. Title: World of golf.
    GV981.M55   1992
    796.352—dc20                              92–13913
                                                 CIP

Printed in the United States of America

10 9 8 7 6 5 4 3 2 1

**HALF-TITLE PAGE:** The Old Course, St. Andrews, Scotland
**TITLE PAGE:** Kiawah Island Resort, South Carolina
**THIS PAGE:** Desert Mountain Golf Club, Scottsdale, Arizona
**FACING ACKNOWLEDGMENTS PAGE:** Deering Bay Estates, Miami,
    Florida

# Contents

# Acknowledgments

The great British writer Bernard Darwin, once wrote, "It is no fun writing a book unless you can write about what pleases yourself." Now, having taken great pleasure in writing a brief history of *Town & Country*'s golf and country club reportage, I admit I had a great deal of help and encouragement over the last two years.

A deep and heartfelt thanks to all the staff of *Town & Country*. I especially want to thank the magazine's former Editor in Chief and current Editor Emeritus, Frank Zachary, the last real editor's editor and a true gentleman, for his guidance, generosity of time, and emotional support. Every writer should be so fortunate.

My deepest appreciation to John Cantrell, the magazine's acting editor, for reading parts of this manuscript, and for so carefully polishing my prose over the last half dozen years; to Melissa Tardiff, the magazine's former art director, who aided in the final selection of photographs; and to a variety of people who read parts of the book to ensure further accuracy: William T. Ketcham Jr., Kenneth A. Menken, Nathaniel Reed, Elliott E. Vose, and William Walton III.

Further research was done by S.J.W. Gordon at the American Antiquarian Society; Art Miller at Lake Forest College; Marilyn F. Traum at the *Chicago Tribune*; Helena Tempest in New York; Laura Stanell at the Pinehurst Convention and Visitor's Bureau; and Steve Schroeder at Robert Trent Jones II. My deepest thanks to all.

Anyone writing about golf today can't effectively do so without the assistance of the United States Golf Association. Thanks to the following there: Karen Bednarski, Diane Chrenko Becker, David Earl, David Eger, and Andy Mutch. Thanks also to the folks at the Time, Inc. photo lab: John Downey, Rob Ritchie, and Eric Valdman.

Along the way, many others unselfishly contributed. Thanks to Slim Aarons, Hugh Best, George "Peter" Bostwick, Ben Crenshaw, George Eberl, Jack Fogarty, Ross Goodner, Bill Hensley, Marcena Hopkins, Gerard Hurley, Rees Jones, Robert Knowles, Patrick J. Leahy, Mr. and Mrs. Theodore E. Loud, Robert MacDonald, David Pearson, Jim Ponce, Lowell Schulman, Nancy Smith, Robert Sommers, Sean Sullivan, Desmond Tolhurst, Rayburn Tucker, and especially Herbert Warren Wind.

Lastly, my sincerest gratitude to Jim Donovan, Taylor's Senior Editor, who believed in the concept of this book, refined it, and generously and thoughtfully added his creative ideas to make it better. His patience, sensitivity, great editorial skill, and sense of humor made working with him a joy.

# PROLOGUE

In 1996, *Town & Country* will celebrate its sesquicentennial, which, in the long roll call of American periodicals, makes it the oldest continuously published general-interest magazine in the United States. The magazine initially was known as the *Home Journal.* In its first editorial, it announced "to the circle around the family table . . . our aim will be to instruct, to refine and to amuse."

By 1850, the magazine had become so established that Horace Greeley, who once advised young men to go West, wrote in the *New York Tribune* that in everything related to taste and fashion, the *Home Journal* was "justly an oracle." The magazine's first editor, Nathaniel Parker Wills, said he edited the magazine for America's "upper ten thousand."

In the 1880s, with more people in America owning more wealth and more leisure time than ever before, and with the greater availability of train and steamship travel, the magazine switched to a society emphasis. The time was ripe. There was the emergence of such social playgrounds as Long Island's North Shore, Saratoga, Newport, Southampton, East Hampton, Bar Harbor, and later Palm Beach and Boston's North Shore. If the magazine seemed rooted in the Northeast, it's because that's where the money was.

This also was a time when golf, country, tennis, and yacht clubs started. There was a renewed interest in hereditary societies: The Society of the Cincinnati, the Sons of the American Revolution, the Society of Colonial Dames, and the Daughters of the American Revolution. Eventually 134 such societies would emerge.

In 1887, there appeared a book in which the so-called best families of the United States were listed, with their full names, addresses, telephone numbers, maiden names, and wives' names by previous marriages, as well as clubs, colleges, summer residences, and yachts. It was an immediate triumph. The book's title was *The Social Register.*

It could be a brutal time trying to break into the stratosphere of American society. Once, at a party given

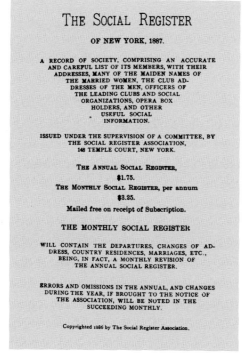

2

by the grandest of Boston's Grande Dames, Mrs. Jack Gardner, a young woman was introduced to her who foolishly tried to impress her by saying that she was a descendant of no fewer than thirteen passengers on the Mayflower. "Well," replied Mrs. Gardner, "I understand our immigration laws are a lot stricter nowadays."

As the last century drew to a close, the magazine continued to define its audience as people "who keep carriages, are subscribers to the opera, have a town house and a country house, give balls and parties." They disapproved of splashy hotels, which threatened to lure people away from the hearth. In 1901, to suggest a wider scope, the magazine changed its title to the pluralistic and catchy *Town & Country,* and soon its pages were filled with social news from around the world.

No magazine in the history of America chronicled the fables and foibles of society so faithfully and fully as *Town & Country.* In words, drawings, and photographs the magazine depicted the worlds of the wealthy, from their grand apartments or houses in the city to their country estates, simple cottages, yachts, gardens, and clubs—wherever the magic wand of their wealth produced a fashionable and high quality of life.

From season to season, year after year, and decade after decade for more than a century, generation after generation of many of the same families replenished the magazine's pages. They included the Adamses, Aldriches, Armours, Astors, Biddles, Bostwicks, Cabots, Cadwaladers, Crockers, Curtisses, DuPonts, Forbeses, Fords, Frelinghuysens, Gardners, Goelets, Goulds, Harrimans, Kahns, Klebergs, Lehmans, McCormicks, Mellons, Morgans, Pews, Phippses, Pratts, Rhinelanders, Rockefellers, Roosevelts, Schiffs, Searses, Stanfords, Strauses, Swifts, Tafts, Van Rensselaers, Vanderbilts, and Whitneys.

In the toll of time and taxes, some families were replaced by others who had acquired a great amount of wealth and had invented a distinct lifestyle. Along the long path to social elevation, they learned one important social lesson—that it takes great style to live a civilized life.

Sport has always been part of the lifestyle of the magazine's audience. Polo, fox hunting, steeplechase, and flat racing have vividly filled the pages of the maga-

---

**ABOVE, TOP.** A 1913 *Town & Country* cover featured a reproduction of "Child Playing Golf" by Bartholomeus van der Helst (1613–1670). **ABOVE.** The 1887 first edition of *The Social Register.*

---

**PHOTO PAGE viii.** The site of six British Opens: Royal Birkdale Golf Club in Southport, England, and its 184-yard, par-3 12th hole.

zine. Tennis, squash racquets, even court tennis have been covered, as well as sailing and skiing. Occasionally there have been articles on football, baseball, cricket, and soccer.

Golf has inhabited a very special niche in *Town & Country*'s history. The magazine has covered the game for more than a century since it published its first golf article on October 16, 1889:

> The game of golf—a pastime formerly almost peculiar to Scotland, and looked upon in that country as a national recreation, has latterly been established south of the Tweed, as well as in many of the British colonies, and ladies have gone in for this amusement, and several ladies' golf clubs have been started. . . . An exact eye, a steady hand, and a strong arm are necessary, and together with the muscular exercise, there is a mixture of walking from hole to hole which, on a fine day, and on an open, breezy common, is very enjoyable and invigorating, and probably accounts greatly for the popularity of the game and the devotion of its votaries to it.

One of the magazine's first golf writers was Horace Hutchinson, winner of the 1886 and 1887 British Amateur. Later Hubert Reed wrote about the latest courses and new champions. In the 1930s the great Bernard Darwin of *The Times* of London wrote several articles, as did Paul Gallico. In the 1940s and 1950s Herbert Warren Wind of *Sports Illustrated* and *The New Yorker*, considered the dean of America's golf writers, contributed four articles.

However, no one wrote more about the breadth and depth of the game for the magazine than a man with two literary given names: H.J. (Henry James) Whigham. From 1910 to 1935 he was editor-in-chief of *Town & Country*. He knew the game as it was played at its highest level of competition; a two-time U.S. Amateur champion, his only equal among national champions as a prose writer was Bobby Jones. He was the author of four books. The first, in 1898, was *How to Play Golf*. He later wrote *The Persian Problem, Korea and Manchuria*, and *The New Deal: English and American*.

Whigham could have been a hero straight out of a Robert Louis Stevenson novel. Like Stevenson, he was born in Scotland, of a prosperous family. He graduated from Queen's College, Oxford, in 1893. He was urged to come to America in the summer of 1893 by Charles Blair Macdonald—who had befriended his father during their days at St. Andrews University—for the Columbian Exposition in Chicago. Along with his fellow Oxford graduates he would show Americans what golf was all about. He stayed on to help H.J. Tweedie and James and Robert Foulis design the course at the Onwentsia Club in Lake Forest, Illinois. In 1896 he became the drama critic for the *Chicago Tribune*, and an instructor in English and Economics at Lake Forest College. In July of 1896 he competed in the second U.S. Amateur that was played at Shinnecock Hills Golf Club in Southampton. He not only was medalist but won it, a rare feat. The following September, he successfully defended his title at the Chicago Golf Club and became the first of only nine champions to successfully defend their championship.

From 1898 to 1905, he served as a war correspondent. He covered the Spanish American War (where his unit was captured), for the *Chicago Tribune* and *The London Standard*. With such noted British writers as Rudyard Kipling and Sir Arthur Conan Doyle, he covered the Boer War, this time for *The London Morning Post*. For them, he also covered the Boxer Uprising and the Russo-Japanese War. From 1906 to 1907 he was the foreign editor of *The London Standard*. He returned to the United States in the summer of 1907 and helped his friend Macdonald in laying out the National Golf Links of America, and he even did some remodeling on the course at Morris Country Golf Club. Later that year, Whigham's good friend Macdonald became his father-in-law when he married Macdonald's daughter, Frances.

As a great sportsman, Whigham took over the helm of *Town & Country* at just the right time. From dawn to dusk he, along with dozens of other editors, writers, and photographers, helped to glorify the Golden Age of Sport. The heroes and heroines of the sporting world filled the pages of the magazine, either in the milieu of their championship seasons, or when, like so many beads of mercury, they were drawn to the heat of society's playgrounds.

This era also was known as the Golden Age of Golf Course architecture, as 75 percent of the greatest

3

**4**

**ABOVE.** Sportswriter Walter Trumbull; H.J. (Henry James) Whigham, national amateur champion in 1896 and 1897 and for twenty-five years editor-in-chief of *Town & Country*; Charles Blair Macdonald, amateur champion in 1895 and Whigham's father-in-law; and architect John W. Cross. **RIGHT.** *Town & Country*, October 3, 1914: Sir John Watson Gordon's portrait of nineteenth-century golf legend John Taylor.

courses in the United States were designed during this time by such golf course architects as Donald Ross, A.W. Tillinghast, Alister Mackenzie, George C. Thomas, Herbert Strong, and Charles H. Macdonald. Such courses included Pebble Beach Golf Links, Cypress Point Club, Marion's East Course, the East and West Courses at Winged Foot Golf Club, Brook Hollow Golf Club, the Upper and Lower Courses at National Golf Club, the North Course at Los Angeles Country Club, Canterbury Golf Club, and Seminole Golf Club.

Whigham wrote about all of these with a romantic and literary flair, often referring to the sea, Shakespeare, and even to Roman mythology. When writing about Cypress Point Club he praised the course highly; what he loved most was that it hugged the ocean, and he wrote, "The tang of the ocean is the breath of the game." When describing the ninth hole at National Golf Links of America, he referred to the forest of trees to the right: "The forest, like Birnam Wood, has taken to marching and moving away to the right. . . ."

When writing about the Indian Creek Club in Miami, where the founding members had dug a golf course by draining a mangrove swamp, Whigham wrote, "When Minerva burst full panoplied from the brain of Jupiter she did nothing more extraordinary than the founders of the Indian Creek Club at Miami Beach."

Whigham was even less objective when writing about his father-in-law's work. He constantly used the National Golf Links of America as the template to which he compared new courses of other architects. At times Macdonald's magniloquent manner was too much for Whigham. After Macdonald designed the wonderful course at Yale University, and was boasting about it, Whigham gently criticized him by writing, "The trouble with Charlie Macdonald is that he never mastered the passive verb."

Whigham also was a fine editorial writer who often took views contrary to the norm. During World War I he praised the Western Golf Association for continuing to conduct their golf tournaments. He was an anti-isolationist, and when it wasn't a popular movement he supported the women's suffrage movement.

In 1925 The Hearst Corporation purchased *Town & Country*, and it became one of the integral cornerstones of its communications empire. Today, under various divisions, The Hearst Corporation is the world's largest publisher of consumer monthly magazines with sixty-one editions in eighty countries; it also owns and operates six radio stations, six network-affiliated television stations, twelve daily and five weekly newspapers, two book companies, and has extensive operations in television production and cable programming.

From the late 1930s until the mid-1960s, the magazine's editor-in-chief was Harry Bull, a man whose taste was comparable to *The New Yorker*'s Harold Ross and *Vanity Fair*'s Frank Crowninshield. Under Bull's stewardship, the magazine took on a high cultural emphasis, and featured the work of some of the best writers of the time: George Bernard Shaw, Ernest Hemingway, Jean-Paul Sartre, Albert Camus, Mary McCarthy, William Saroyan, Evelyn Waugh, and Jean Cocteau. In the October 1950 issue the magazine serialized Waugh's *Brideshead Revisited*.

In the fall of 1972 Frank Zachary was hired as the magazine's editor-in-chief. He brought to his position a deep well of talent and a wide breadth of knowledge and experience. During World War II he had co-developed *USA* and *Victory* magazines. He had been the East Coast editor of *Modern Photography*. He had also published *Portfolio* for the graphic arts. Although only three issues were produced before it ceased publication, it's considered one of the greatest achievements of modern-day graphic publishing. From 1951 to 1964 he was the art director of *Holiday*, where he created the concept of environmental portraiture—the use of a person in a photograph with a related subject. It rocked the world of editorial photography.

Zachary slowly changed the magazine's focal point to a successful blend of national and international society, with an emphasis on trends in fashion and graceful living. He integrated a monthly social and cultural calendar, expanded the wedding and party sections, and added a wonderful dash of highbrow humor. In the magazine's commitment to recognizing social obligation, in 1986 it established the "Generous American" award, honoring exceptional American philanthropists.

5

The new look was highly successful. During Frank Zachary's nineteen-year tenure, until he retired in the fall of 1991, the magazine's circulation tripled, and gross revenues increased tenfold.

Though he wasn't a golfer, he knew the game and had a strong appreciation for its history and traditions. In 1935, for the *Pittsburg Bulletin Index*, he covered the U.S. Open at the Oakmont Country Club. The championship was won by Sam Parks Jr., a young, local club professional, who was the only one in the field to break 300 for four rounds.

It was a victory filled with as many ironies as the Oakmont greens are with breaks. Parks never again would scale the heights to win a national championship. In fact, he remained a rather obscure club professional and later a salesman for U.S. Steel Corporation. However, the reporter for the Index would go on to become a great magazine art director and later editor-in-chief. His editor—who knew something about country club life—would go on to become one of America's most famous twentieth-century novelists. He was John O'Hara.

My association with *Town & Country* began in the spring of 1973. I had completed four years as an associate editor of a golfing publication, where a staff of five somehow turned out a highly readable and entertaining magazine every month. I had grown up in a golfing family in northeastern New Jersey and was exposed to the game and championship courses at an early age. My maternal grandfather played, and on Sundays after church we would join him at his club for lunch. My mother and father also played, as did my aunt and uncle.

My first assignment for *Town & Country* was to write about Shinnecock Hills Golf Club in Southampton, New York. The club's president had granted me permission to write about the club, and a friend was a member. With some expense money the magazine had given me I went out for a week's stay. It was early May, before the Southampton season began, and the course all week was less crowded than usual, meaning on any day there were only two rather than four foursomes playing.

While our foursome stood on the first tee, perched high above the fairway, I wasn't sure if I was being taken on a playing tour of the grand course or simply being taken. Though I always like to play for a friendly wager, the traditional bet we made on the first tee seemed to me rather low. Thus, while observing, asking questions, and taking notes, I soon forgot about the bet. A gross tactical error. I wasn't reminded of the bet until I missed a small par putt on the par-3 17th hole and my partner winced and said, "That was an expensive miss." When we finished the round and went to the Jefferson Bar, I quickly discovered how expensive my errors had been. There had been automatic "press bets," press bets on top of press bets, and individual bets. In the span of three and a half hours I had lost half of my expense money. But I got the story, and Frank Zachary liked my work.

From then on I followed green fairways across the country, around the world, and back in time. On the par-5 9th hole at Muirfield in Scotland, I was walking toward where my fourth shot had landed when my caddie stopped about three yards right of my ball and said, "Right here, sir. This is where Mr. Cotton's second shot landed during the final round when he won The Open here in 1948." That Mr. Cotton got there in two and that I lay four didn't seem to matter. I was on historic turf. It could have been the Old Course, Troon, Royal Lytham & St. Annes, Royal St. George's, Royal County Down, Royal Portrush, Winged Foot, or Augusta National— each course's past, in which great deeds had been accomplished by great champions, seemed to gallop in tandem with the present.

I've sipped port in the clubhouse of the Royal and Ancient Golf Club and looked out over the marvelous linksland that make up the Old Course, the New, the Eden, and the Jubilee. I've had lunch at National Golf Links of America, I've eaten ginger snaps at Seminole Golf Club, and I've stood on the 16th tee at Cypress Point overlooking the Pacific with a driver in my hand about to hit into a strong wind. Yes, I made it across, but just.

I discovered through the years that it was the memorable people I met who marked the progress on my own psychic map.

When I was in England in 1976 I had the memorable experience of talking with Lady Heathcoat-Amory, better known as Joyce Wethered, who was Britain's fin-

6

est female golfer. Even now, with the welcome rise of women's golf and its many skilled practitioners—and decades after she first made her mark—Joyce Wethered is considered the equal of Babe Didrickson Zaharias and Mickey Wright.

In only seven years of major competition in the 1920s, Joyce Wethered won the English Ladies Championship five straight times and the British Women's Amateur Championship (the premier event of the day) four times. However, her reputation rests on her scoring. At a time when women were just about breaking 80 she was consistently scoring near par.

While women admired Joyce Wethered, men adored her. Prior to the 1930 British Amateur she played an informal round with Bobby Jones, her brother Roger, and Dale Bourne over the Old Course at St. Andrews. There, playing from the championship tees, and in a breeze, she shot a dazzling 75. Of her round Jones wrote, "She did not miss one shot; she did not even half miss one shot; and when we finished I could not help saying that I had never played golf with anyone, man or woman, amateur or professional, who made me feel so utterly outclassed."

As for her feelings about women and golf, she once wrote, "I am not talking about ladies' golf, because strictly speaking there is no such thing as ladies' golf at all—only good or bad golf as played by members of either sex."

Having been beaten myself by several women who played very good golf, the statement spurred a question in my mind about golf between men and women, or more specifically, about men and her. But Lady Amory, as I would call her, doesn't like to talk much about herself. She is incredibly modest. In her living room in the small cottage just off the mansion of her estate in Tiverton, Devon (now owned by the National Trust, it includes a beautiful 25-acre garden), there's not one trophy photo or book that would indicate England's finest female golfer resides there.

She greeted me dressed in blue trousers, a pale pink-and-white gingham blouse, an orange wool cardigan, and wearing a strand of pearls. Her eyes were a soft hazel; her white hair was short and brushed back. Her handsome good looks belied her age. For at

"Oh, Beautiful World." Editor-in-chief Frank Zachary, as depicted by Arnold Roth.

8

Joyce Wethered *(left)* and Glenna Collett Vare during the first Curtis Cup match in 1932.

seventy-seven she was extraordinarily attractive. Close to six feet tall, her posture was wonderfully erect, her walk brisk. But her most engaging feature was her smile. When she smiled, which was often, she radiated a feeling of complete self-fulfillment and a spirit absent of guile.

I thought it untimely to ask my questions about golf between the sexes, so I asked her how she learned the game.

"Oh," she said, smiling, "I learned by copying. My father used to take Roger and me to watch golf when we were youngsters, and I tried to copy the good players' rhythms. Then when I began playing fairly well I played a lot with Roger and his friends from Oxford." (Roger Wethered and his Oxford friends didn't exactly play off a 15 handicap. His friends were Cyril Tolley and Ernest Holderness. Between them they won the British Amateur five times and played on twelve Walker Cup teams.)

Though I then felt I could ask the question I'd patiently waited to ask, I'm vulnerable to women with warm smiles; I hesitated, and only asked Lady Amory if she still played golf. She replied that she hadn't played in ten years, and had even forgotten where her clubs were, but admitted she watched all the golf she could on television. I asked if she had watched the Colgate European Open for Women at Sunningdale. Yes, she had. Then I asked what she'd thought of last year's winner, Chako Higuchi, who has a finely tuned sway in her swing. "I would like to see her play in the wind," she said sententiously.

"How does one avoid swaying?" I asked.

"Your only hope," Lady Amory said, smiling, "is to keep your head absolutely still."

I was troubled. It wasn't because I have a difficult time keeping my head absolutely still during my swing, but because I was having a difficult time imagining Lady Amory grim-faced in a fierce duel, her hazel eyes icy, staring in putts and staring down opponents. She didn't appear to have that desperate competitive edge evident in so many great champions. Her manner was gentle and placid. And because of this I asked her how she approached competitive golf.

"I always took golf as a game," she answered,

"not as the most important thing in my life. You've got to be able to enjoy it, or it is not a game."

"Were the major competitions enjoyable?"

"The championships were not enjoyable."

"But your incredible record. . . ."

"Oh," she said with a modest smile, "I loved to play golf right. Once on the course I never looked back, never looked forward, but played in the moment."

That's it. Her secret, apparently as simple as slipping on a golf glove, but as difficult to achieve as trying to keep the left arm straight during the backswing. Play in the moment.

A slight drizzle was falling, and I asked to see her garden; then I had to leave. Being a dedicated gardener, Lady Amory was delighted it was raining, delighted I wanted to see her garden and, I feel, delighted I would be leaving. We walked past the thirty-foot-high trimmed hedges of the formal garden, then ambled through acres and acres of informal garden. She pointed here and there to an incredible variety of plants and flowers she had planted the year before or ten years ago, telling me their names. All too soon I was at my car, where she gave me directions on how to get on the motorway and to Surrey. "Lady Amory," I asked, "did your late husband, Sir John Heathcoat-Amory, ever beat you playing golf?" I knew full well he was not a golfer of her stature.

"Oh yes," she said, "I remember the first time he did. Later we were driving home from the club and he somewhat absent-mindedly said, 'I didn't play very well today.' And then he looked at me and realized what he had said. It was a very odd moment for both of us."

I reflected upon this—the supreme tenderness these two people were strong enough to show and feel toward each other. Nothing more was said. I shook her hand. It was a pleasant ride to Surrey.

Another great amateur golfer I spoke with was Charlie Coe. It was in the summer of 1984, and he was at the Castle Pines Golf Club outside Denver, which is now the annual site of The International tournament. From the late 1940s to the early 1960s, Coe was not only one of the best amateurs in the country, he was one of the best players. He won two U.S. Amateurs, was runner-up in the 1951 British Amateur, played on six

9

10

**ABOVE.** Charlie Coe en route to the 1958 Amateur Championship.
**RIGHT.** Byron Nelson.

U.S. Walker Cup teams, and in 1961 missed by a single stroke tying Gary Player for the Masters. "Golf," he told me, "is a game of mental gymnastics."

He spoke about the final of the 1959 U.S. Amateur held over the East Course at the Broadmoor Golf Club in Colorado Springs, where Jack Nicklaus beat him 1-up in one of the greatest finals in the history of the U.S. Amateur. The quality of play was very high, and the match shifted back and forth several times. By the time both reached the 36th hole, the match was all even. Both men drove well. For his second shot, Coe hit a splendid eight-iron shot, but the ball rolled off the green into some rough. Nicklaus played a nine-iron and put the ball seven feet left of the pin. Coe then hit a beautiful pitch and the ball rolled and rolled down the green and just stopped short of going in. He had his par.

"I'll tell you," Coe said to me, "I didn't like Jack. Sure he was good. Real good. But he was rather arrogant. I really didn't like him, and we didn't talk much during the finals. On the last green Jack had marked his ball. He was replacing his ball and I signaled to him and conceded the putt. I knew he was going to make it. Then Jack looked at me and said, 'No, Charlie, that's not the way I want to win.' Of course he holed the putt. But from that moment on I changed my mind about Jack."

By the time I began looking for heroes, Byron Nelson already had quit competitive golf except for an occasional tournament. I did get to see him play a few holes in an exhibition, but that was in the early 1970s and he was in his sixties and long past his prime. The champion who was in his prime as I was growing up was Ben Hogan. He, indeed, possessed the great stuff of heroes. He was a great golfer who had survived a near-fatal automobile accident and had returned a greater champion. Whenever he came to New Jersey I went to see him play, especially at the U.S. Open at Baltusrol Golf Club.

Naturally, when I was researching an article on golf in Texas I wanted to talk with Hogan. I wrote him. He answered my letter and graciously explained that he no longer gave interviews. I wanted to talk with Byron Nelson, but I hesitated because he was going through a very difficult time. His wife Louise had just suffered a stroke which would later prove fatal, and at the time she was completely comatose and being watched around the clock by nurses at Byron's home.

But my friend Ben Crenshaw said he would speak with Byron. He did, and told me that I should call Nelson for an appointment. I did, and a few days later I drove out from Fort Worth to his cattle ranch in Roanoke. Since I once had written an article on pure-bred cattle breeding, I knew the difference between a Hereford, a Brahman, and an Angus.

Byron couldn't have been more gracious and generous with his time, considering the circumstances. We talked for some time, and after an hour and a half he looked at his watch and said, "Now Dick, I can give you five more minutes. Then I must go in and look after Louise. Although she's completely comatose, every two hours I go in and hold her hand. I know she knows I'm there by her."

Five minutes later I was at the door, and we shook hands. He turned away, then came back to the door and asked, "Do you know how to get back to Fort Worth?" I told him I did. One is never too old to find new heroes.

The idea for a *Town & Country* golf book began brewing half a decade ago. When I studied the magazine and researched its back issues, I felt like a golf course architect asked to design eighteen holes over a beautiful terrain of 500 acres. Like the architect who could fit three courses in the terrain, I realized there were at least three *Town & Country* books.

I knew that the book would have to embrace the magazine's long and historic golfing tradition, society, and lifestyles. The emphasis would be on lifestyles featuring social playgrounds with their tribal mores, sports, and clubs. Since the magazine has covered dozens of such playgrounds in over a century, my criteria for inclusion was twofold: each place would have to have been covered continually by the magazine for at least half a century, and each would have to be a place where the game of golf had flourished. This eliminated such places as Newport; although the first U.S. Amateur and Open was played at Newport Golf Club in 1895, golf never flourished there until the 1930s and then only for a decade. It was better known for its sailing and tennis, although in the last decade golf again has flourished. At

11

Saratoga and Aiken and Camden, golf was played in the 1890s, but they are predominantly famous for their equine sports.

The social playgrounds I have included are Pebble Beach, Palm Beach, Palm Springs, the Carolina Sandhills, and the Hamptons. For almost a century, hardly a winter or summer season has gone by that the magazine hasn't covered some function in Palm Beach or the Hamptons. The youngest playground is Palm Springs. It was founded in 1931, not initially as a golfing playground but for tennis, when Charlie Farrell and Ralph Bellamy founded the Racquet Club. Golf began its historic rise there in the early 1960s.

Both Pinehurst and Pebble Beach get covered every decade or so, and have been a major part of America's golfing landscape for ninety-five and seventy-three years, respectively. While geographically they couldn't be more different, they are alike in many ways. Both possess a sandy soil that is wonderful to walk on, excellent for drainage, and ideal footing for equine sports. Both resorts have helped to nurture golf for men, women, amateur, and professional. And both have played host to national championships and will continue to do so. In 1994 Pebble Beach will be the site of the U.S. Amateur and in 1995 Pinehurst No. 2 will be the site of the Senior Open. Each has a lifestyle both highly civilized and glamorous.

Country clubs have been part of the lives of *Town and Country* readers for more than a century. This realm of good manners and high courtesy, with its tidal repetition of form and tradition, continues to generate a unique mystique in the social order. After all, country clubs remain, at least ostensibly, one of the few social status symbols money alone can't buy. Gaining membership in the right club still can secure and elevate a person socially, and that person will gladly help perpetuate the club's traditions. That clubs don't change is a fallacy. Clubs do change in small and subtle ways and usually against the grindstone of the past. Of course, it would almost be an act of heresy for clubs to publicly announce that they do in fact change. Silence is one of their strongest powers. Thus, I think the myths and realities of country club life deserve their own chapter in this book.

Since so much of the appeal of *Town & Country* is visual, I also decided that the book should include a collection of "best of" photos in color and black and white, illustrations and cartoons. For the three parts of this book I searched through 75,000 photographs. I hope you like the ones selected.

As *Town & Country* approaches its sesquicentennial, it will continue "to instruct, to refine and to amuse the circle around the family table." And it will successfully continue to anticipate and report on the changing trends in society, lifestyles, culture, fashion, and high finance. While the writing will be more provocative, it will be no less polite, always respecting our readers' sensibilities and good taste.

# *TOWN & COUNTRY's* GOLFING CAPITALS OF AMERICA

# THE HAMPTONS

Out on Long Island's south fork, past the potato fields and beyond the trendy ways of Southampton's Job's Lane, are those fabled cheek-by-jowl clubs: Shinnecock Hills Golf Club, National Golf Links of America, and Maidstone Club. Nowhere else in America are there three better private clubs for golfing in the same small crease in space.

Here among the tall grasses twitching in the breeze, among the wind-seared sand dunes, you'll find a grand tradition of championship golf. Here among the minutes of annual meetings, some now dating back a century, you can read how these clubs helped nurture golf in its infancy in the United States. Here, in the words that the late Alfred Wright wrote in *Sports Illustrated* more than a decade ago, is the "Last Bastion of Elegance." This quality permeates the clubs from their carpeted locker room floors, up their cleat-marked staircases to the main rooms where old British golfing prints grace the walls.

For great championship golf at a true family

golf club, there is Shinnecock, many of whose members also belong to Southampton's other two specialized clubs: The Bathing Corporation and the Meadow Club for tennis. National, as well known for its great food as for its golf, boasts a membership roster that could make up a corporate *Who's Who in America* and resembles a British men's club where women and children are merely tolerated. Maidstone, the social center of East Hampton, is a sporting triple treat, offering within one club first-rate golf, great tennis on grass courts, and a splendid beach facility with a pool and cabanas. Like the clubs, each clubhouse is distinctive and reflects the genteel era that bred them.

Shinnecock's clubhouse sits high on a hill exposed to the winds sweeping in off Peconic Bay and the Atlantic Ocean. It's the very first clubhouse built in the United States, completed in 1892 and designed by Stanford White. It's an unpretentious medium-sized building with brown shingles and white wood trim. White Ionic columns march down its open porches. It looks as

18

though it might have been the modest summerhouse of Samuel L. Parrish, one of the club's founding members.

By contrast, National's clubhouse is an opulent, sprawling building of beige stucco and green shutters. In front is a formal garden with a fountain featuring a caddie with clubs in one hand and a champagne glass in the other. The screened-in porch near the front door boasts a three-foot-long telescope, a reminder of those halcyon days when the club manager had to identify the approaching yachts of members and prepare for their docking at the club's marina. The marina is gone. Now members and their guests approach the club along a circuitous road that stops at the club's entrance, which is marked by two huge iron gates. Inside is a sign warning motorists to kindly halt if golfers are putting on the nearby 17th green or driving off the 18th tee.

Within the clubhouse are murals of the Old

---

ABOVE. Weekend golf at Shinnecock around the turn of the century.

---

PHOTO PAGE 14. The 490-yard, par-5 13th hole of the Maidstone Club in East Hampton, New York. OVERLEAF. The 425-yard, par-4 18th, the green of the 418-yard, par-4 9th, and the clubhouse of Shinnecock Hills Golf Club.

Course at St. Andrews and of the club's founder, Charles Blair Macdonald, the winner of the first U.S. Amateur in 1895. The large windows of the main dining room overlook Peconic Bay. The comfortable living room is pine paneled, with bookcases, a fireplace, portraits of golfers, a bronze bust of Macdonald and overstuffed leather chairs. It's an ideal place to be alone with a snifter of cognac while contemplating life's stymies.

At the end of a long and winding road, sitting hard by the Atlantic Ocean, is Maidstone's Tudor-style clubhouse. In the summer gloaming it looms up like a grand nineteenth century English estate mansion, perhaps in Maidstone, England, the town for which the club is named. On the clubhouse's long terrace overlooking the Atlantic and in its ballroom, painted a soft peach color, there's an ambience of formal informality, as with most family-oriented clubs. But more impressive is the feeling that there will be no intrusion here on one's privacy.

At this trinity of clubs, the right to privacy as an essential condition of life hasn't been eroded by the rigors of time. For over seventy-five years, a policy of shunning publicity has been as carefully maintained as the greens and fairways. True, all three courses are currently listed in *Golf Digest*'s America's 100 Greatest Golf Courses (Shinnecock 4th, National 34th, and Maidstone 57th). That's viewed as more than enough publicity.

Only six times in their history have these courses entertained a national or international competition. The second U.S. Open and Amateur were played at Shinnecock in 1896. The 13th U.S. Senior Amateur was held at Shinnecock in 1967; in 1977 it hosted the 26th Walker Cub Matches, and in 1986 it held the U.S. Open. It will host the centennial U.S. Open in 1995.

Maidstone never has hosted even a state championship. And it probably never will. Aside from the fact that the course is slightly too short for today's long hitters, one of the club's long-standing bylaws is that no working photographers be allowed on club grounds. Even members and guests aren't encouraged to take photographs at the club.

Because of the 1986 U.S. Open, Shinnecock gets more attention than the other two clubs, and it ranks high among the list of great golf courses. It can handle it. To discourage too many guests, the fee for guests unaccompanied by a member is $125. That's without the caddie or golf cart fee. They can only play Tuesdays, Wednesdays, and Thursdays, and the number is limited to sixteen. Then there's the club's general manager, Henry Nichols, an officious gentleman whose mind ticks like a computer gleaning information from cross-references. He knows, but will not tell you, who just married or divorced whom, who is the cousin, ex-wife, husband, or uncle of whom. "I don't care," he says, "if Jack Nicklaus walked in and wanted to play the course. I would say, 'Mr. Nicklaus, who is your sponsor?'"

Although Shinnecock has a very affluent membership, by mid-summer the clubhouse looks as if it could use a fresh coat of paint. The boards are loose on the porch. The men's locker room looks as though it was installed in the 1920s—and it was. The course has a shaggy wind-blown look about it. All this is intentional. For Shinnecock represents the finest understatement of wealth that money can buy.

During the summer the club serves only one meal and that's lunch. Since a dozen years ago when one woman said, "Shinnecock is a great club to belong to, but you can find better food at the Southampton Diner," the club has made a concerted effort to upgrade its food. "Now," says the club's current president, Elliott E. Vose, with as much pride as if he had just birdied the club's 6th hole, "members sometimes come to the club just for lunch." The menu includes such culinary staples as a ham and cheese on rye sandwich (no butter) and hamburgers. Recently, pasta dishes have been added, as have crab cakes and a caesar salad. And there's hardly a better view on the East End than sitting on the club's back porch and gazing over the 9th green, the 18th fairway, and in the distance, part of National's course and Peconic Bay.

Still, while other clubs usually have a concession stand somewhere on the course where the golfer can pick up a much-needed Bloody Mary, a cold beer, a hot dog, or a bowl of chili, Shinnecock doesn't have one. In fact, nowhere on the course is there even a portable toilet. But that's Shinnecock. "If you can't last nine holes," says a woman member, "you shouldn't be playing golf."

Yet if a guest makes disparaging remarks about such spartan surroundings—the bleak windswept course with its acres of rough, heather, small pepperidge trees, and 139 bunkers (Augusta National has only 88)—and wonders why a blanket of fog is covering the course at 9:30 A.M., a member will simply retort, in a voice that sounds as though his sinuses were stuffed with pâté, that if you don't like it, go home. Go over to The National. This isn't ultra-snobbism; it's merely a statement that these links represent golf as it should be.

Shinnecock is a harsh course, devastated by constant winds and haunted by the old concept that the natural terrain and elements are the best hazards, that golf is a game played in the air; where the emphasis always should be on shotmaking, not putting, and where you should literally tack your way down the fairways into a wind or crosswind.

From the back or red tees, the course measures only 6697 yards (the course was lengthened 215 yards for the 1986 U.S. Open), and plays to a severe par 70. From the green or regular tees, the course measures 6243 yards, and from the white or the ladies' tees just 5306 yards.

The hardest hole on the course is the par-4 473-yard 6th. It's called the Pond, as it has the only water on the entire course. "Wait until you play the sixth," is the usual remark from a member. In fact, the golf hole was so revered by one member that when he passed on, his

19

will stipulated that his ashes be spread over the 6th green.

The hole swings slightly right. The tee is nestled among some pepperidge trees. From the back tee it's a 250-yard carry to reach the fairway. Making matters worse, the area with rough between the tee and the fairway is raised, creating a blind tee shot. Just where the fairway swings right, there's a huge sand bunker that will catch a badly pushed or sliced drive. Farther down the left side of the fairway there's a cluster of four bunkers that come into play for the really long hitters and when the hole is playing downwind. From these bunkers the fairway dips slightly downhill to the pond that occupies the right half of the fairway. From there, the ground rises fifty yards to a small flattish green guarded on the left by a large shallow bunker. Behind the green is deep rough and pepperidge trees. During the 1986 U.S. Open, the hole played to a stroke average of 4.64.

In the 1960s, before the course even was considered for the 1977 Walker Cup Matches and the 1986 U.S. Open, Ben Hogan played the course twice with his friend and member Paul Shields. He played under the most difficult wind—an east wind. He scored 71 and 74. High for Hogan. Yet he later wrote Shields, "Although Shinnecock is a very old course, it has not succumbed to the pattern of 'make golf easy' because of the hacker's inability to hit decent shots. To me, Shinnecock affords any golfer a most pleasant eighteen holes of golf. By this I mean each hole is different and requires a great amount of skill to play properly. As I think back, each hole has complete definition. You know exactly where to shoot and the distance is easy to read. All in all, I think it is one of the finest courses I have ever played, and I can say that I had a great amount of pleasure the day we played there."

Hogan's letter was written before an irrigation system was installed and the rough was allowed to grow as high as an elephant's eye. Ah, what rough. Pity the plight of a golfer participating in a Seniors tournament here in the early seventies. On the 16th hole (the second of the two par-fives), he hit a long drive that hooked just slightly into the rough. "Can I get home with a two?" he asked his caddie. "Sir," replied the caddie, "you'd be better off if you just pitched the ball back onto the fair-

**20**

way." Not heeding the caddie's advice, the man hit his two iron. The result: two broken ribs.

It's such rough along with the plethora of bunkers that has led the learned host of so many PBS programs, Alistair Cooke, to write, "My own private conviction is that Shinnecock was designed by Lady Macbeth."

Not quite. However, a case of mistaken identity of the original designer has almost as many twists as a Shakespearean plot. For almost a century it was believed that Willie Dunn, a Scottish golf pro, was the original designer. This legend had been perpetuated when club member Samuel Parrish stated that the pro they hired from the Royal Montreal Golf Club to design the course was Willie Dunn. In fact, the person was Willie Davis, who would also design the original course at Newport Golf Club. Davis designed the original twelve holes at Shinnecock. When they became too congested, he designed an additional nine holes just for women. However, that nine was abandoned in 1892. Six holes were added to the original twelve and these, it's now assumed, were designed by Willie Dunn.

The course was completed in 1892. Although it wasn't the first 18-hole course in the United States— that distinction belongs to Chicago Golf Club— Shinnecock was the first club to have a waiting list. And it was one of the first clubs to welcome women as regular members.

And they proved themselves worthy of their petticoats. The first U.S. Women's Amateur was played at the Meadow Brook Club, and was won by Shinnecock member Mrs. C.S. (Lucy) Brown. She shot 69, paused for lunch, then played the back nine in 63 for a nifty total of 138. The next three Women's Amateurs were won by Shinnecock member Beatrix Hoyt, the first of the great female teenage athletes and the granddaughter of Salmon P. Chase, Secretary of the Treasury under President Lincoln. She retired from competitive golf at the age of twenty.

In 1931 Shinnecock's course emerged as it is today. Since the original layout was in the path of the expanding Sunrise Highway (Route 27), a parcel of land west and north of the clubhouse was obtained. The club hired the firm of Toomey & Flynn to design the new

Willie Davis, the designer of Shinnecock.

22

**ABOVE.** Early Shinnecock member Beatrice Hoyt, three-time Ladies Amateur Champion, with clubhouse in background. **RIGHT.** The victorious 1977 Walker Cup team at Shinnecock.

course. William Flynn had designed the Cascades Course at The Homestead and Cherry Hills Country Club. The firm's construction engineer was Dick Wilson, who would become one of America's most prominent golf course architects, designing such courses as Doral's Blue Course, Bay Hill Club, and the original course at La Costa.

The course has withstood the test of time and the assault of modern golf equipment. From 1973 until the U.S. Open in 1986, the non-competitive course record from the championship tees was a five-under-par 65 by Ben Crenshaw. (The competitive course record of 63 was set during the Open by Chip Beck.) After Crenshaw played the course in 1973 he was asked if he thought Shinnecock would be a legitimate course for the U.S. Open. In his response, Crenshaw proved not only to be a keen prophet but also attuned to the club's feeling of fealty to the past. "You bet," he said. "It would be great. And there should be no television towers. A U.S. Open from Shinnecock should be on radio."

In June 1986 the modern world of golf and television descended upon Shinnecock for the U.S. Open. For many Southamptonites it was an unwelcome intrusion upon their privileged world. Fearing their town would be jammed with people and massive traffic jams, many stayed away for the week and even put their houses into a rental pool, hoping to reap a huge financial gain by renting them out to the television executives or the contestants and their retinue. They had few takers.

Better the Southamptonites had stayed and come out to watch the Open. It was a wonderfully organized championship. Because Shinnecock is open only seven months, from April to October, and has such a small membership, the United States Golf Association simply leased the club for a week, paid the club $500,000, and took over the complete operation of the championship itself.

The traffic engineers and the Suffolk County police did such a good job that even on the final day the traffic flowed smoothly. A huge footbridge was erected over Highway 27 to get the spectators to and from the course to the parking lots.

To prepare for the Open the club created five new tees: on the par-5 5th, the par-4 6th, the par-4 9th (but it was never used), the par-4 13th, and the par-5 16th. Still at 6912 yards it was the second shortest course after Marion East to have the Open in the 1980s.

During the practice rounds, the contestants realized that the wind—the cleanest hazard of all—was going to be the determining factor. The winds blew up to 20 miles an hour. Playing downwind one day on the 472-yard 12th, Jack Nicklaus used a driver and a nine-iron to reach the green. When the hole played into the wind, he needed a driver and a full three wood to reach the green.

As the competitors tacked their way down the fairways during their practice rounds they discovered another of Shinnecock's more subtle features. It was neither the holes that played directly into the wind nor the downwind that presented the most problems, but rather the holes that played into the crosswind. That put a premium on proper club selection and shotmaking.

The first day of play began overcast with a northeast wind sweeping in off the Atlantic. By late morning the sky had darkened and the wind had picked up. The mood was foreboding, and when the haunting sound of a train whistle pierced the air, it seemed more like the western coast of Scotland than the eastern coast of Long Island.

Suddenly a northeaster whipped in. Winds gusted up to 40 miles an hour; the rain, pushed by the wind, fell more horizontally than vertically. Play was suspended for nineteen minutes. By day's end the scores more resembled those of a British Open than the U.S. Open. Bob Tway, who finished just before the rain delay, posted the lowest score of the day, an even-par score of 70. It was the highest first-round Open score since the 1974 Open at Winged Foot Golf Club.

Jack Nicklaus toured the front nine in one over par. On the 10th tee, with the wind in his face, he hit a high drive. The wind caught the ball and pushed it far right into the sea grass. Nicklaus, his caddie, and some of the gallery searched for the ball. Just before the regulation five minutes were up, Nicklaus declared the ball lost. (He later said it was the first time since the 1959 British Amateur that he'd lost a ball in tournament play. Surely, another Nicklaus record.) Then, like many a golfer before him, he took the long and lonely walk back to the tee. He made double bogey on the 10th and two

23

more double bogeys to finish at 75. The average score of the day was 77.55.

The following day, the weather had cleared and the winds lessened. The scores came down. Greg Norman led with a one-under-par 139. The 36-hole cut was 150. A nineteen-year-old amateur, who had shot an 88 the first day, bettered his score by twelve shots on Friday, but still missed the cut by twelve shots. His name: John Daly.

Although on Thursday the gallery had been small, for the last three days of the championship the maximum number of 18,000 (the course could have handled 5000 more) spectators a day came out. Even the Long Island Railroad—never known as one of the more efficient railroads in the country—outdid itself and brought in 1100 New Yorkers.

While the incoming nine plays sixty-six yards shorter than the outgoing nine, its tumbling and twisting fairways and plateaued greens make it a much more difficult nine. During the first two days of Open play it yielded only 80 birdies and collected 126 bogeys. As with most major championships, the Open was going to be either won or lost on the incoming nine.

Midway through the final round on Sunday as many as nine golfers were either tied or within one shot of the lead. As Raymond Floyd made the turn, his wife Maria looked into her husband's blue-green eyes. She told a friend "he had the look." It was a look a dragon slayer would envy, focused and fiercely determined. As other players faltered, Floyd's game excelled. On the uphill par-3 11th, he holed an eighteen-foot putt for a birdie 2. At the par-4 13th, he stuck his second shot within four feet of the pins and holed that putt for a birdie 3. On the long, par-5 16th, he put his third shot eight feet above the cup and holed that putt for a birdie 4. On the par-3 17th, he struck a splendid four-iron shot that held into the crosswind and ended up twelve feet from the pin. He just missed his birdie putt and then squeezed his next putt in for a par. He parred the final hole. Floyd had birdied three of the last eight holes for an incoming nine of 32 to go with his outgoing nine score of 34, a 66. He was the only player to break par for 72 holes and his margin of victory was two shots, over Lanny Wadkins and Chip Beck.

Shinnecock proved a great venue for the U.S. Open. It had a worthy winner in Raymond Floyd, winner of two PGA Championships, a Masters, and twenty-one tournaments on the PGA Tour. The contestants in a rare chorus of unison praised the course as very hard but fair. And even the old and wind-blown money people of Southampton, once they realized the spectators were more interested in golf and were neither going to drink their whiskey nor steal their silver, enjoyed the championship. Shinnecock's members in their own understated manner took an enormous and justifiable pride in showing off their grand jewel to the golfing world.

In 1995, during the year-long centennial celebration of the United States Golf Association, the U.S. Open will again return to Shinnecock. That year its next-door neighbor, National Golf Links of America, will be celebrating its 87th birthday. When National opened in 1908 it was to be the ultimate golf course. Nothing less would do for its creator, Charles Blair Macdonald. Macdonald, a man with an ego as large as the 250 acres on which he built National, was the winner of the first U.S. Amateur in 1895. He admitted to being a male chauvinist, and passionately hated people who argued over the often murky rules of golf, stating that perfect justice would make for a dull and dreary game. For thirty-one years he was the autocrat at National to such a degree that National often was referred to as "Charlie's Club."

While a great deal has been written about National, even by the architect Robert Trent Jones, who once wrote, "Charles Blair Macdonald sowed the seeds of modern golf-course design," the best work on why National was created was written by H.J. (Henry James) Whigham, from 1910 to 1935 the editor-in-chief of *Town & Country*. The last article Whigham wrote for the magazine appeared in September 1939; it was titled "The Evangelist of Golf." It was about Macdonald, who had just died, and while of course Whigham was biased toward Macdonald, he placed the importance of National in proper historic perspective:

The elderly gentlemen who took to golf in the early '90s because it was fashionable soon discovered that they could not compete with the experts at all. A missed shot with the old 'Gutty'

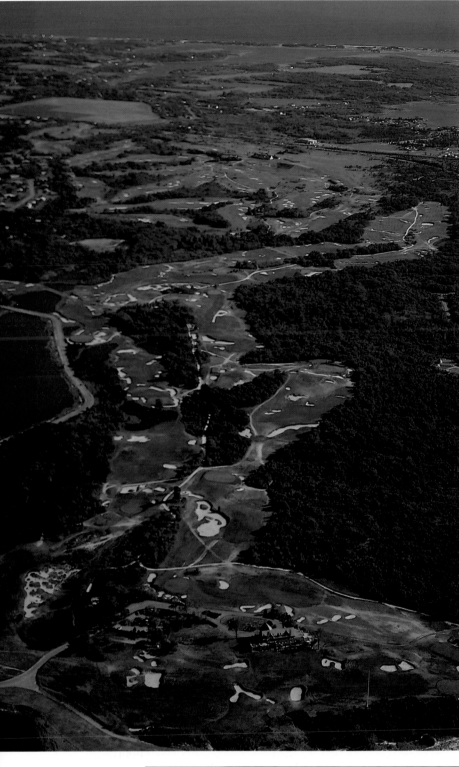

**ABOVE.** All this golf. Aerial view of Shinnecock Hills Golf Club and National Golf Links of America, Southhampton, New York. **ABOVE RIGHT.** Ray Floyd, winning the 1986 Open.

ball went nowhere, but it did knock up the face of the wooden club and tear the skin off the fingers. So golf gradually began to lose its devotees. . . . The invention of the rubber-cored ball by Haskell in 1898 came just in time to save the game. Inferior players found that the new ball was much easier to hit and was certainly less destructive of clubs and hands than the old gutty. From that time on golf began to flourish as the ideal sport for the incompetent. And there I believe it would have remained if it had not been for Charlie Macdonald. . . .

Pondering the grievous depths to which American golf had sunk, Macdonald conceived the idea of building a truly great links which would so change the minds of golfers that they would never again put up with the miserable game to which they were accustomed. With this in view he traveled to England and Scotland to pick out eighteen holes of Britain's great seaside courses. . . .

He did not, it is true, reproduce eighteen classic holes. The holes he copied in detail were the Redan at North Berwick, the Alps at Prestwick, and the Eden and the Road holes at St. Andrews. . . . Several other holes at the National have features borrowed from Littlestone and Muirfield and elsewhere. But it very soon became apparent to Macdonald, once he had picked his ground on Peconic Bay, that nature, here too, had her own suggestions, and it was far better, and certainly much more amusing, to utilize features of the land than to copy slavishly from the great masterpieces.

Indeed what Macdonald actually accomplished was finer than what he had originally planned. He did produce a course with eighteen great holes, and in doing so created masterpieces of his own which have been reproduced in many parts of America.

National is steeped in egocentric Macdonaldisms. During the 1920s he fired a greenkeeper who called the front part of the 5th tee "the ladies' tee." Until the 1970s, a sign on the first tee read, "Ladies are permitted to play on the course by courtesy and should be accompanied by a member of the club. Such matches must always step aside and allow properly constituted matches to pass, regardless of position on the course."

To this day the main dining room is for men only. The same is true for the club's fourteen guest rooms on the second floor. "Ladies," says club manager Randall Herring, "haven't stayed here since the war."

In the 1920s, a member approached Macdonald and suggested it would be nice if a windmill were put up beyond the 17th tee. Macdonald agreed, had it done, and then put the complete cost of the project on the member's monthly bill. The member paid the bill.

The greatest Macdonald story that has made neither the history books nor the record books concerns golf's most expensive golf shot. In the early 1930s Macdonald's nephew, Jay Peter Grace, who retired as president and CEO of W.R. Grace & Company, approached his uncle and claimed that he could drive the green on the first hole, a par four measuring 301 yards. Macdonald was adamant that it couldn't be done. To prove he was right, he gave his nephew three tries. Grace's first two shots fell short. But on his third shot he hit a booming drive that bounced onto the green and rolled twenty feet past the pin. An infuriated Macdonald, seeing his course demeaned by a single stroke, turned on his heels, walked into the clubhouse, called his lawyer, and had his nephew stricken from his will. The amount was reputed to be over half a million dollars.

Also in the 1930s, Macdonald tried to steal away Shinnecock's golf professional Charlie Thom, who had been at the club since 1906. In no uncertain terms Thom told Macdonald what he thought of him. "I wouldn't be there ten minutes before I would wrap this golf stick around your neck and make a bow tie for you." Thom stayed happily at Shinnecock as its professional and in various other capacities for over seventy years.

However, Macdonald was successful in stealing away Shinnecock's chef and in inaugurating superb cuisine, which has become as famous as the course. Lunch is the meal. It begins with either clam chowder or clam bisque, followed by a cold one-pound lobster and fish cakes; the entrée can be either beef or kidney pie or shepherd's pie, a veal dish or filet of beef, followed by rice cakes smothered in cinnamon and maple syrup.

Neither Shinnecock nor Maidstone have challenged National's supremacy of cuisine. And that's one of the few things Southampton and East Hampton hap-

26

**TOP.** The first U.S. Amateur Championship at match play at St. Andrew's Golf Club in 1895. The winner, Charles B. Macdonald *(center)* is flanked by *(left to right)* James Park, Lawrence Curtis, George Armstrong, and Louis Biddle. **ABOVE.** Shinnecock member Ridgely Harrison. **LEFT.** A 1916 *Town & Country* illustration of Charles B. Macdonald, winner of the first U.S. Amateur in 1895 and founder of National Golf Links of America.

28

**ABOVE.** Looking back toward the clubhouse at National from above the 17th tee. To the left is the 2nd green and to the right is the 1st green. **RIGHT.** The tough 402-yard, par-4 uphill 9th at Maidstone.

pily agree upon. The residents of both towns have carried on a friendly rivalry for over a century. In unkind moments the residents of East Hampton refer to Southamptonites as "new rich" and "new social" and refer to themselves as "old rich." To counter, a favorite Southampton line is that "those who live in East Hampton would really prefer to live in Southampton." So it goes.

East Hampton always has attracted a more "artsy" crowd. It was where the artist Jackson Pollock lived. The great sportswriter Grantland Rice summered there. Actress Dina Merrill always summered there. And within the last decade more actors and actresses have come out, such as Kathleen Turner and Chevy Chase and director/producer Steven Spielberg. The latter quickly learned that the fame of Hollywood celebrities carried little clout in East Hampton.

Early one summer evening Spielberg and two of his assistants were in a pizza parlor just up the street from the movie theatre. Like everyone else they were standing in line to get their order and a table. One of Spielberg's assistants grew impatient and went over to the proprietor and politely asked, "Is it possible for us to be seated and served?" He then added what was to be his downfall. "You know," he said, "you have movie people here." The proprietor looked at him and retorted, "We get movie people all the time. We get them from the seven o'clock show and the nine o'clock show."

The village of East Hampton is quaint, with two- and three-storied white clapboard buildings with shingled roofs. Church steeples soar above the treeline. It's all placed in a pastoral setting around a village green and a pond known as Georgica Pond. The main thoroughfare in the village is appropriately named Main Street. Off of it are narrow, winding, tree-lined roads.

The Maidstone Club is situated one mile east of the village on some 280 acres, and is surrounded by expensive homes. The club was founded in 1891. For almost the first quarter century of the club's existence its tone was set by its first president, a paternalistic, benevolent man named Dr. Everett Herrick. He was a God-fearing Methodist. He allowed some of the land he owned adjoining the club's grounds to be used as part of the golf course, rent free. His only stipulation was that there was to be no golf on Sunday.

When the club purchased the land in 1905, the Sunday golf ban was lifted. Golf could be played, but not until after 12:30, by which time it was hoped that those golfing members had made peace with the Almighty.

Herrick was also a health-food addict and teetotaler. When he died in 1914, he bequeathed Maidstone $7500 with the condition that if intoxicating beverages were ever sold on the club's grounds, the legacy would revert to the East Hampton Free Library. With the repeal of prohibition, an anonymous member promptly sent the club a check for $7500. Soon the Maidstone bar became as well-stocked as the public library.

In fact, day in and day out during the summer some of the best shots at Maidstone are poured at the bar, usually in the form of the members' favorite drink, a Southside: one ounce of either gin, vodka, or rum with lemon juice, sugar, and a sprig of mint.

Maidstone's initial thirty-six holes were designed by John and Willie Park. It was Willie Park, winner of two British Opens in the 1880s, who was part of the first wave of great Scottish professionals who turned to golf course design.

The club's first eighteen holes, which is the main course, were completed in 1899. It wasn't until 1925 that the Park brothers' second design of eighteen holes was completed. During World War II, when the club was strapped for funds, nine of those holes just east of the clubhouse and running along the sand dunes were sold off.

In 1965 the architect Alfred Tull added some new tees to the main course. Still, Maidstone isn't a long course. In fact, it's one of the shortest great courses in the country. From the championship tees it only measures 6332 yards and plays to a par 72. The distance is deceiving. There's Hook Pond (so named because it's shaped like a gigantic fish hook) that comes into play on five holes. On four of those holes you must hit your tee shot over it. The 5th and 7th greens jut fiendishly into the pond.

As with Shinnecock and National, there's the wind. The prevailing wind is a southwest wind off the Atlantic. When it comes sweeping in, the par-5 490-yard 13th hole running up toward the beach is hardly reachable with three wood shots. The 9th hole, which looks

29

**ABOVE, TOP.** The seaside mood of Maidstone. A lone golfer tacks his way up the 13th fairway. **ABOVE.** *Town & Country* cover girl Ina Lunde summering in Southampton.

for all the world as if it were imported from Royal Birkdale in England, usually plays into a crosswind. Although only 402 yards, it plays longer. The fairway sits in a fold of two long sand dunes. The green is plateaued. To the right of the green is a mammoth hollow of sand and dune grass. The members refer to the hollow after one of their favorite football stadiums—"The Yale Bowl."

But where the course truly becomes memorable at Maidstone is from the 7th through the 10th holes. No less of an authority than Bernard Darwin, *The Times* of London golf correspondent who played the course in 1922, said, "The seventh through the tenth holes is the finest stretch of consecutive holes in the United States." The 7th is a short par 4 that swings around Hook Pond. The golfer can cut off as much of the pond as the nerves allow. A bold drive across the pond will leave a pitch shot to the green that hugs the pond.

The green of the short par-3 8th is surrounded by sand and tucked among huge sand dunes. The 10th hole is a longish par 4 that runs in the opposite direction of the 9th; its green is perched with an inglorious security on top of a sand dune. Playing these holes has the same emotional impact on the golfers as a visit to the dentist's office.

Last year, both Maidstone and Shinnecock celebrated their centennials. However, they aren't the oldest clubs in the Hamptons. Such distinctions belong to both Meadow Club, founded in 1887, with thirty-nine grass tennis courts—it has more grass courts than any other club in the country—and the Quogue Field Club. Although the latter has moved from its original location, it offers both tennis and golf, but only nine holes, as nine holes were wiped out during the hurricane of 1938.

Actually, the next oldest club is the Westhampton Country Club founded in 1890. The Southampton Golf Club, adjacent to Shinnecock, began in 1925. There are three nine-hole courses, two of which are public: the Sag Harbour golf course, which up until 1987 still had sand greens; the Amagansett golf course; and the private Bridgehampton Golf Club. In Montauk there's the daily-fee Montauk Down golf course designed by Robert Trent Jones. The last club formed was the Noyac Golf Club in Sag Harbor, which opened in 1961.

The hot golf talk of the Hamptons this season is about the latest golf club: The Atlantic Golf Club. It's in Bridgehampton seven miles inland, covering what once was farmland. The club's story is about the right man being in the right place at the right time.

But it's a narrative spun by a plot of love and romance and the stuff of summer dreams. The dream began more than fifty years ago. In the summers of 1940 and 1941, Lowell Schulman was first introduced to golf as a caddie at Winged Foot Golf Club in Mamaroneck, New York, in the shadow of the majestic Tudor-styled clubhouse and the two championship golf courses and the aura of championship golf. All this made an indelible impression on the teenager. Schulman was not the kind of boy who grew up to be a championship player. In fact, his lowest handicap was seven. But he did grow up to be a real estate tycoon who now owns and operates twenty-six buildings in White Plains in Westchester County, New York.

In 1963 he was the original developer of the Brae Burn Country Club in Purchase, New York. And for the last forty years he has been a member of the Old Oaks Country Club, also in Purchase.

Over the years, acquaintances took Schulman to play golf at both Shinnecock and National. Just a few hours at each was enough to stir Schulman's imagination.

In 1988 Shulman was divorced and dating Dianne Wallace, a woman who adored the beaches of the Hamptons. Friends asked them out for a weekend. As if moonstruck, Schulman suddenly became enraptured with the romantic lore of the Hamptons, the beautiful beaches and dunes, the cooling sea breezes, and the chic summer social life.

As a golfer, Schulman knew it would be almost impossible to gain membership into Shinnecock, Maidstone, and National. They are essentially closed clubs, not closed to Jews—each club has some members who are Jewish—but closed in the sense that they take in fewer than half a dozen new members yearly and each has a long waiting list.

Schulman wasn't the only one. There was a strong demand for another club. "I didn't even do a marketing study," says Schulman. The next week he was out in search of a suitable site. He found 204 acres of what

31

had been poor farmland. Poor, because it was gently rolling with ridges and plateaus. But it was ideal for a golf course. But was it available? For decades, Suffolk County has been buying the development rights of farmers, to keep the Hamptons an agrarian environment. Fortunately for Schulman, the land he wanted hadn't been sold. That was the first of two lucky breaks. The next stroke of luck was that there were artesian wells.

Schulman then hired Rees Jones as the architect. Jones was basking in the glow of just having successfully done some redesign work at The Country Club for the U.S. Open. The youngest son of golf course architect Robert Trent Jones, he grew up in the business. He learned to play golf at the Montclair Golf Club, a splendid and very traditional Donald Ross design that has been the site of the U.S. Amateur and Women's Amateur. He was highly familiar with the sandy soil and the wind patterns of the Hamptons, having been the construction engineer at his father's design for Montauk Down. He has had his own firm since 1982.

Schulman bought the land for $7.5 million. The next step, and one that has caused the downfall of the most tenacious developers, was getting the approvals of several boards: The Southampton Town Planning Board, the Suffolk County Health Department and all its subdepartments, and the New York State Department of Environmental Conservation.

The whole process is analogous to a jockey running a steeplechase course. Danger lurks everywhere, and the wrong move at the wrong time can mean disaster and a doomed project. It demands deftness, intelligence, and endurance. It was a lengthy process that took almost a year, but in the end Schulman's lawyer negotiated the course with all the skill of a hero in a Dick Francis novel.

Construction began in March 1990 involving earth moving, shaping of the fairways and greens, drainage, a very sophisticated irrigation system, and fi-

nally, seeding. It took until October. The greens and fairway are bent grass, the first rough of rye blue grass, and the heavy rough is fescue.

Although surrounded by trees, the course itself is treeless, very much like a Scottish course, with hummocks and craggy swells. "There's some wonderful elevation," says Rees Jones. "In fact from several tees, you can see the Atlantic Ocean. I created several cathedral holes where the fairways are set in a valley of huge mounds. I would call this a friendly course. The fairways are amply wide, and there are four par four holes under 400 yards." The course measures 6840 yards and plays to a par 72. In October 1991 the course opened for four days, as a sort of membership drive. The whole cost of the project, not including a clubhouse now going up, was $30 million.

As of January 1992, the initial membership of 160 members had been filled. Each member put up a refundable bond (but no interest) of $125,000. Annual dues, exclusive of the annual food and beverage allowance, is set at $7500—on the high end of New York metropolitan clubs.

"All the members have a reverence for golf, are like-minded, and have the financial ability to afford the club. For many, it's a second or third club. We have regular women members. They can play anytime," says Schulman.

In the spring of 1990, Schulman married Dianne Wallace and purchased a summer home in East Hampton. "My wife," he adds with an ironic smile, "still prefers the beach. In fact, I'm beginning to enjoy the beach."

The shingled clubhouse is nearing completion, and the course is getting rave reviews. Schulman has discovered, like generations before him, that the Hamptons have the magical power to be able to sift even the summer sands of daydreams of over fifty years into solid, golden realities.

33

LEFT. The 433-yard, par-4 16th hole of the Atlantic Golf Club, the newest course in the Hamptons.

# THE CAROLINA SANDHILLS

In the south central region of North Carolina, in what are known as the Carolina Sandhills, are the two small towns of Pinehurst and Southern Pines. They occupy no more than twenty-five square miles of land, and have a total population of less than 15,000, even during their season from October to May. Combined, the towns possess one of the highest incomes per capita in the state, yet both towns intentionally remain beyond the loud chorus of commercialism.

For this is an area that aspires to be nothing more than what it is—a place that quietly suggests a more placid time in America, before people began to take life on the run. Even the land rolls gently, like the sea rippled by a benign breeze.

In the spring, the morning sunlight filtered through the pines has an almost iridescent glow. The countryside serves up a profusion of blossoming white and pink dogwood, azaleas, camellias, and magnolia trees. The warm dry air, so healthy to breathe, so sensuous to the skin, is velvety soft. The tall trees and sandy soil carpeted with pine needles so muffle sound that at times the only noise is the peaceful whisper of pines in the breeze.

Although the Sandhills are seventy miles south of Raleigh and one hundred twenty miles northeast of Wilmington, the terrain seems coastal. Millions of years ago there was an inland sea here, not unlike California's Salton Sea, that slowly receded and left the sandy soil. More than seventy years ago several of the area's oldest families—the Tuftses from Boston, the W.O. Mosses from Savannah and Durham, and John Watson from Chicago—discovered the real wealth here was in a land fertile for their sporting passions.

The sports they brought here are their legacies. Those who share a passion for golf (The Sandhills have thirty courses with two true championship courses), fox hunting, the breeding and training of hunters and jumpers, steeplechasing, and flat racing and trotting have populated the area. There always has been a friendly, healthy rivalry between the golfers and the

**ABOVE, TOP.** Pinehurst in the spring: the 18th tee of the No. 2 Course. **ABOVE.** Dorothy Campbell Hurd Howe with her son Sigurney on the links at Pinehurst. **RIGHT.** Mrs. Estelle Lawson Page lofts the ball over a rock at Pinehurst at the 1941 Women's North and South. She won it a record seven times.

**PHOTO PAGE 34.** A golfer's second shot has to carry the stream in front of the green on the 439-yard, par-4 5th hole at Pinehurst National Golf Club.

horse set. The golfers often speak about the fox hunting crowd by quoting Oscar Wilde: "The unspeakable in pursuit of the uneatable."

The people here have formed a society that's as paradoxical as the terrain; while many come from the middle South, the society has inherited some proper Bostonian characteristics instilled by old Boston families who came here more than seventy years ago seeking a more moderate winter climate. They set a tone of cordial reserve, reverence for the past, and a strong sense of tradition. Many of the older residents' voices contain a faint Boston accent tinged with a slight southern drawl. They still refer to The Pinehurst Hotel by its original name of some seventy years ago—The Carolina—but they pronounce it "The Cah-o-lina."

With its winding roads and lanes, the soaring steeple of the village chapel, and the colonial-style buildings of red brick with white wooden trim, Pinehurst looks as if it had been plucked whole from the New England countryside. The very name Pinehurst suggests a New England heritage. In the 1890s the Tufts family vacationed in the summer on Martha's Vineyard. A real estate developer there was conducting a local contest for the best name of his new development. One of the names submitted, but not used, was Pinehurst. The Tufts liked the sound of the words and felt it perfectly evoked their land of tall pines and the sandy soil.

Even the moral atmosphere of Pinehurst was established within the resort's first decade of existence. Before the village chapel was built, Sunday sermons were preached in the town hall by the famous Boston and Harvard Unitarian minister, Edward Everett Hale. And soon the New England conscience became as pervasive as the tall pines. In essence, the New England conscience doesn't stop you from doing what you shouldn't; it just stops you from enjoying it.

Further proof that golf is a game of moral fortitude, of almost transcendental dimensions, is the fact that these residents of Pinehurst have been playing and enjoying it for almost a century. Although golf was played at other resorts in America before it was played in Pinehurst, no other resort helped to popularize and spread the game by honoring its past, enhancing its present, and envisioning its future better than Pine-

hurst. In 1962, when the U.S. Amateur finally was played over the famed Pinehurst's No. 2 course, one sportswriter opined, "This is as appropriate a gesture to history as it would be to play the World Series at Baseball's Hall of Fame in Cooperstown, N.Y."

One family and one man are mainly responsible. The family was the Tufts, and the man was golf course architect Donald Ross. Their partnership was one of the happy accidents in golf. In the 1880s, a Bostonian named James Walker Tufts was amassing a sizable fortune developing a drugstore chain. In 1891 he consolidated his firm with the American Soda Fountain Company and became one of the first men to successfully develop a feasible method of quadruple silverplating.

At the time, Tufts was fifty-six and not in robust health. He had visited the Sandhills and he felt its rejuvenating climate would be ideal for him and other people of moderate means who wanted to escape the harsh northeastern winters. From July 1895 to December 1896 Tufts purchased 6947.75 acres of cut-over timberland for $9100 from the Henry Page family. When

Tufts bought the final parcel of 5980 acres at just over a dollar an acre, Mary Page, sister of Henry Page, found out about the transaction and told her brother, "As much as I dislike these Yankees, it's inexcusable to have gouged them in this way."

But with that unrelenting Yankee pride, Tufts was determined to make something of the area. On his very next visit he brought with him plans for a town. They had been drawn up by the landscape architect Frederick Law Olmsted, designer of New York City's Central Park (with Calvert Vaux), Brooklyn's Prospect Park, Chicago's Jackson Park, and the landscaping for the Biltmore Estate in Asheville, North Carolina.

Olmsted's plan called for a village common with a town hall at one end and a church at the other. The streets would wind around a village green. In 1896, when the Holly Inn was completed, Tufts sent out notices to Northern doctors saying, "Consumptives are welcome." It was then believed that tuberculosis was hereditary. The next year, when it had become known that tuberculosis was contagious, Tufts sent out notices reading, "Consumptives excluded." Until 1970 the

**38**

deeds to houses sold to future Pinehurst residents specified that no one with tuberculosis could buy a house, making Pinehurst one of the few resorts in the world where discrimination was practiced on the basis of health.

In 1898 Tufts noticed some people hitting golf balls over a few makeshift golf holes. He ordered a nine-hole course built, and a year later, another nine. Two years later Tufts realized what he had. And he persuaded Donald Ross to come down for the winter as the resort's professional.

Ross was born in Dornoch, Scotland, in 1872. He studied golf and clubmaking under "Old" Tom Morris at St. Andrews. In 1893 he returned to Dornoch and became the greenkeeper and golf professional at Dornoch Golf Club, and he studied grass and golf course design under the tutelage of the club's secretary, John Sutherland. In 1898 a Harvard professor of astronomy, Robert Wilson, was visiting Dornoch and persuaded Ross to emigrate to Boston. The trip cost most of Ross's earnings, and he arrived in Boston with only $2. Wilson got Ross a job as the pro and greenkeeper at Oakley

Country Club in Watertown, Massachusetts. The Tufts were members of Oakley during the summers. Ross returned to Oakley as its pro and later the Essex Country Club.

Initially, as a golf course designer, Ross had several advantages going for him. The sandy soil of the Sandhills was very reminiscent of Dornoch. There also was plenty of water for irrigation and a plentiful work force. In all, Ross designed seven courses in the Sandhills: four at the Pinehurst Country Club, and a course each at Southern Pines Elks Club (1910), Mid-Pines Resort (1921), and Pine Needles Country Club (1928). In a career that spanned fifty years Ross and his associates designed over three hundred courses. At the peak of his career in the 1920s, Ross had a winter office in Pinehurst, a summer office in Little Compton, Rhode Island, and branch offices in North Amherst, Massachusetts, and Wynnewood, Pennsylvania.

1900 proved to be a momentous year for James Tufts. In the spring, Harry Vardon, who had at that point won three of his six British Open titles, was in the United States giving a series of exhibitions. He played four rounds over Pinehurst's No. 1 course. With his effortless swing and consistent play, Vardon hoped to give the game the kick of popularity it needed in the Sandhills. That December Ross arrived. He immediately redesigned the No. 1 course. In 1901 he began on Pinehurst No. 2. It was to be his masterpiece. In 1907 the full eighteen holes opened. Ross would redesign the course four more times, the final time being in 1934 when he changed the greens from sand to grass. He later described it as "the fairest test of championship golf I have ever designed."

What will never be known—whether it was intentional or unintentional—is why Ross never gave No. 2 a signature golf hole (although uphill the 438-yard par-4 5th almost qualifies, it doesn't), something like the 16th at Cypress Point, the 10th at Winged Foot West, or the 18th at Doral's Blue course. A hole to which photographers with their telescopic lenses flock, and the golfer stands on the tee with the awful feeling of foreboding that either he or she is about to take a triple bogey.

When one thinks of No. 2, it is as part of the complete golf course, in that no part is greater than the

---

ABOVE. Leonard Tufts and Donald Ross. RIGHT. The 1st green of the No. 5 Course, and in the background the grand clubhouse of the Pinehurst Country Club.

40

**ABOVE.** The 1951 U.S. Ryder Cup team *(left to right):* Jackie Burke Jr., Ben Hogan, Ed Oliver, Jimmy Demaret, Henry Ransom, Sam Snead (captain), Lloyd Mangrum, Clayton Heafner, Skip Alexander, Dutch Harrison. **RIGHT.** Labron Harris *(left)* accepts his trophy for defeating Downing Gray *(right)* to win the 1962 U.S. Amateur Championship at Pinehurst. USGA President John Winters *(center)* congratulates them. **FAR RIGHT.** Denny Schute, winner of the 1936 PGA at Pinehurst.

whole. Indeed, no two holes are at all alike, yet each fits perfectly into the puzzle. And because the fairways are shielded from one another by tall pines, each hole takes on a lonely character of its own. The fairways are deceivingly wide yet a drive placed on the wrong side of the fairway will make it almost impossible for the golfer to get the ball on the green let alone close to the pin on the approach shot. Then there are the very strategically placed fairway bunkers and the bunkers guarding the crown-shaped greens. They're small and filled with subtle contours and flow beautifully into the fairway, making the course a sublime chipping course without equal in the United States.

For ninety years, generation after generation of America's top-ranked men and women amateur golfers have had the opportunity to play No. 2 under tournament conditions. Since 1909 it has been the site of the North and South Amateur. The tournament actually began as early as 1901 and was originally called the United North and South and played over the No. 1 course. The first official Women's North and South was played in 1903; that also was the first year of the North and South Open Championship, which was played until 1951.

No. 2 was the site of the 1936 PGA Championship, the 1951 Ryder Cup Matches, the 1962 U.S. Amateur, the 1980 World Amateur Team Championship, and the 1989 Women's Amateur. In 1994 it will be the site of the Senior Open. From 1973 through 1982, No. 2 was the site of the World Open, later renamed the Hall of Fame Classic. Rarely has a golf tournament destroyed the reputation of a course quicker than the World Open. The very character of the course was ignored, and it was set up like any other course on the PGA Tour.

Bermuda rough lined the fairways stopping golf balls from bounding into the pine trees. Rough was allowed to grow around the greens, and because the tournament was held in either August or September, two of the hottest months of the years in the Sandhills, the bent grasses were heavily watered.

Give the touring pros soft greens, and low scores are almost guaranteed. There were 62's and 63's, and the winning score often was 18 under par. The game's purists winced. Over the next nine years No. 2 was

41

slowly restored to its original splendor. In November 1991 the Tour Championship, the final tournament of the PGA Tour that finalized the tour's strategic categories—the Vardon Trophy winner and the money winners—was scheduled to be played there.

The course was in perfect shape. Only light rough was allowed to edge the fairways, allowing an errantly hit drive to bound into expanses of hardpan to nestle at the base of a pine tree or end up on a bed of pine needles. The greens were fast and very firm, and the rough around them was cut, allowing a misgauged shot to roll off the green and down into a small hollow. The golfer was then left with three options: either to putt the ball, hit a pitching wedge, or attempt a chip-and-run shot.

To the surprise of everyone the touring pros, who can be as critical of golf courses as theatre critics are of new plays, unanimously praised the course. At the end of the third round an incident as rare as making a double eagle occurred. Paul Azinger, who had been in contention, ballooned to a seven-over-par 78. He approached Tour commissioner Deane Beaman, and instead of berating the course extolled it. He told Beaman he hoped the Tour Championship would be returned to No. 2 in 1992. It was.

In a playoff against Russ Cochran, Craig Stadler won the tournament with a respectable 8 under par. Pinehurst No. 2 had returned to its former glory as one of the premier courses in the United States. With its graceful, broad fairways lined by regal tall pines, comparing it to newer courses such as the Stadium Course at PGA West with its artificial look, its 17-foot-deep sand bunker, and its island green is like comparing the elegant acting of Audrey Hepburn to the dancing and prancing of Madonna.

No sooner had the touring pros left and the conversation about No. 2 course quieted down, when the sound of hoofbeats could be heard in the Sandhills. Fox hunting season was approaching and the horse set that lives beyond Pinehurst and in Southern Pines were arriving to occupy their houses, which are set back off the main roads behind turned and tooled split-rail fences.

The Moore County Hounds, founded in 1914 by James Boyd, a historical novelist who wrote *Drums* and *Marching On,* is the oldest private pack in the deep South. (Boyd's estate, now called Weymouth Center, with its writer-in-residence program, has become the cultural center of the Sandhills.)

Although the Sandhills don't have the majestic, rich, rolling green terrain of Middleburg, Virginia, or those excellent scenting conditions, it has many advantages. The winters are moderate and there are no biting north winds that pierce through the heaviest hunting jacket. The footing is wonderful for the horses because there are no rocks and no mud.

The hunt season opens Thanksgiving with the annual drag hunt. During the season hunts are held every Tuesday, Thursday, and Saturday. The average field is sixty, and during the season there are between fifty and sixty hunts. The season ends in mid-March with a hunt brunch.

Then the polo season begins: from April to June and then again from September to November. From September to May there's the training of the trotters and the pacers. But the horse event of the year, that brings

people from all over the state in mid-April, is the Stoneybrook Steeplechase race. It's one of the continuing rhythms of the past that's so pervasive in the Sandhills. It began in 1941 when three hundred spectators came out to watch. Now more than 35,000 crowd the race grounds for a festive afternoon of lunching, drinking, and betting. The golfers and the horse set mingle, sharing drinks and betting information.

This is the sense of continuity that even Richard Tufts was proud of. The grandson of James Tufts, Richard Tufts graduated from Harvard in 1917 and after serving in the Navy during World War I, he returned to Pinehurst. He worked for his father, Leonard, through the 1920s, and when his father retired in 1930, he continued as director of Pinehurst, Inc. until the 1960s.

A modest, bespectacled man who consistently scored in the 70's, Tufts's contribution to golf was enormous. He was simply called "Mr. Golf." He served as head of more committees of the United States Golf Association than any other man, and was its president in 1956–1957. He was the guiding spirit behind the formation of the World Amateur Golf Council. In 1963 he was the non-playing captain of the U.S. Walker Cup team. Although his team was down 3 to 6 after the first day of play, he rallied his team and they won 12 to 8.

In 1960 he wrote *The Principles Behind the Rules of Golf,* which still is considered one of the most enlightening books on the subject. When the 1962 U.S. Amateur was played over the No. 2 course, instead of the typical program, Tufts wrote a book titled *The Scottish Invasion,* a brief history of golf and its great players. In the spring of 1992, when Richard Tufts was inducted into the PGA World Golf Hall of Fame, golf historian Herbert Warren Wind commemorated him by saying, "If golf had a Thomas Jefferson, that man was Richard Tufts."

A good friend of Donald Ross, in the 1950s he helped lay out Pinehurst's No. 4 course from the original Ross design. He even showed a flair for golf course architecture when he assisted Ellis Maples with the routing of No. 5. In 1971 the stockholders and most of the Tufts family, who owned the majority of the stock in Pinehurst, Inc., voted to sell the resort to Diamondhead Corporation for $7.6 million. "Except for losing my par-

**ABOVE.** A morning ride for the Moore County Hounds. **LEFT.** Peter Tufts in front of a portrait of his father Richard Tufts.

**OVERLEAF.** The 17th hole at Pinehurst No. 2.

ents," says Richard Tufts' son Peter, "that was the saddest day of my life."

Diamondhead quickly turned Pinehurst into a gristmill for making money. They changed the name of the Carolina Hotel to the Pinehurst Hotel. They built condominiums too close along the fairways of the No. 5 course. They completely changed the character of the No. 2 course. As one resident puts it, "real estate salesmen were as thick as ants at a picnic." However, Diamondhead did build the PGA World Golf Hall of Fame just beyond the 5th tee of the No. 2 course; and they did build the No. 6 course, designed by George and Tom Fazio. Financially over-extended, Diamondhead was taken over by a consortium of banks. In 1984 they sold Pinehurst, Inc. for $20.2 million to the Club Corporation of America, which at the time either owned or operated more than thirty-five country clubs and resorts around the world. The Club Corporation of America seized the moment; it embraced most of the Tufts' traditions and began running Pinehurst more as a resort and recreated a relaxed yet formal ambience. The only real estate property they developed is the new No. 7 course, designed by Rees Jones.

While all this change was going on, the Country Club of North Carolina just down the road from Pinehurst was quietly and carefully establishing itself as one of the premier clubs in North Carolina and one of the best residential developments.

It had been carved out of an unspeakable wilderness. Since the 1920s most of the land had belonged to an eccentric man named John Watson, who invented the automobile's shock absorber. His avocations were golf and nature study. He bought 900 acres of rolling land and dammed three streams that now form part of Watson's Lake. When he died in 1952, the land was put up for sale. The executor of Watson's will was a Pinehurst resident and lawyer, Livingston Biddle. It wasn't long before he thought he had a potential buyer in Richard A. Urquhart of Raleigh. On February 16 Biddle, Urquhart, and Bargrove (Skipper) Bowles Jr., chairman of the North Carolina board of Conservation and Development, made a date to see the land. Mother Nature also made the trip, with a slashing sleet storm. "There wasn't a God-damn nickel's worth of common sense

among us," Urquhart later commented.

A charter membership was formed and the land was purchased for $525,000. Only members could buy land. An additional three hundred acres were also bought. In February 1963 the club officially was formed, and because it was within one hundred miles of four-fifths of the state's population, it was called the Country Club of North Carolina. Urquhart was elected the club's first president, and he ran the club with an iron hand from the discreet distance of Raleigh.

Local golf course architect Ellis Maples was hired to design the first eighteen-hole course, named the Dogwood because of the profusion of dogwood trees on the property. A big course, it measures from 5317 to 7154 yards and plays to a par 72. The course rises up from Watson's Lake over heavily rolling terrain, with longleaf pines and dogwood trees lining the fairways. The terrain offers a wonderful variety of up- and downhill holes. The course has only seventy-five bunkers, but water, in the form of streams, ponds, and lakes, comes into play on ten holes. For regular play the course is hard even though it doesn't demand the precise shot-making of, say, Merion's East or Winged Foot's West Course. But when the course is set up for championship play, with the Bermuda rough allowed to grow and line the fairways and the large, undulating bent-grass greens are shaved and become fiendishly fast, the course is a very stern test.

The course was the site of the 1980 U.S. Amateur. (Because two courses are needed for qualifying, the other course was Pinehurst's No. 2.) In the last week of August, 282 golfers showed up. Among those who made it to the sixty-four qualifiers were many of the perennial amateurs: Jay Sigel, Richard Siderowf, Gary Cowan, Jim Holtgrieve, Allen Doyle, and Don Allen. At least a third of the qualifiers would go on and join the ranks of the touring pros, and now are the backbone of the PGA Tour. There was the defending champion, Mark O'Meara, and medalist Fred Couples. Some of the others were Jodie Mudd, Bob Tway, Mark Brooks, Jim Gallagher, Willie Wood, Brad Faxon, Keith Clearwater, Steve Jones, and Jay Don Blake. The winner, Hal Sutton, beat Bob Lewis 9 and 8.

In 1979, as the club's membership expanded to

over five hundred, another nine holes, also designed by Ellis Maples, were added. Robert Trent Jones was hired to design another nine, which was opened in 1985. Both nines were combined and the eighteen-hole course was named The Cardinal, because of the colorful bird's prominence. Including resident, out-of-state, and international members, the club's membership now exceeds eight hundred.

Halfway between Pinehurst and Southern Pines, on Midland Road, is Mid-Pines Resort where, in the 1950s, Julius Boros once honed his game. Across the street is Pine Needles Country Club, a resort owned and operated by Peggy Kirk Bell. The grand lady of women's golf received the Bob Jones Award from the United States Golf Association for her respect and sportsmanship in the game of golf. Her cozy resort of Swiss-styled chalet-cottages sports an outstanding Donald Ross course. It was the site of the United States Golf Association's Girls' Junior in 1989, won by Brandy Burton. In 1991 it played host to the USGA's Senior Women's Amateur, won by Phyllis Preuss. In 1995 Pine Needles will host the Women's Open. That year Pine Needles will open their new course, designed by Pete Dye. Having a course designed by the subtle Ross next to one designed by the more flamboyant Dye is like having a duet sung by Perry Como and Bruce Springsteen.

By 1995 it's projected that the Sandhill area will have thirty-five courses. Although Pinehurst has been a popular resort area, it was slow to expand. There was a new course built in either the 1930s or the 1940s. One course was built in the 1950s. During the 1960s and 1970s, ten new courses sprang up.

But those two decades paled next to the 1980s, when eleven new courses were built. Jack Nicklaus designed a course for the Pinehurst National Golf Club, and his firm, Golden Bear Design, did the course at the Legacy Golf Links. Arnold Palmer designed the course at the Pinehurst Plantation. Dan Maples, one of two sons of the legendary Pinehurst architect Ellis Maples, was the busiest of all the golf course architects. He designed three—The Pit Golf Links, one of the most exciting courses in the area; a new eighteen-hole course at Woodlake Country Club; and the splendid course at Longleaf Country Club.

**47**

In retrospect it appears that one fine morning a score of developers woke up and proclaimed that they had a brilliant idea for a new development or club that would flourish in the Pinehurst area. Brilliant they were not. They were just geniuses for the obvious.

Almost one hundred years ago Donald Ross told James Walker Tufts an adage as old as the game of golf: "Golf and sand go together." Nowhere is this a richer truth than in the Carolina Sandhills.

ABOVE, TOP. Vicki Goetz, winner of the 1989 Women's Amateur over the famed No. 2 Course, and a member of the 1990 and 1992 Curtis Cup teams. ABOVE. One of the grande dames of golf, Peggy Kirk Bell, at her resort, Pine Needles, site of the 1989 Girls' Junior, the 1991 Senior Women's Amateur, and the 1995 Women's Open.

# PALM BEACH

If Palm Beach were as large as its reputation, it would be a mid-sized continent. Around the world, the very words Palm Beach are synonymous with opulence and glamour, conjuring up a rapturously sunny spot where some of the world's wealthiest and privileged people reside from November until April, and live a lifestyle as sophisticated as a Cole Porter lyric.

Their surroundings resonate to a perfect pitch of easy charm and high-toned elegance. The town of Palm Beach is an enchanted, insulated island with wide boulevards, majestic, tall royal palm trees, Mediterranean Revival architecture, and ubiquitous green and-white-striped awnings. However, for all the town's largess (people in Palm Beach rarely do things in a small way), the town actually is quite small. At its widest it's no more than four rather long blocks, and it's just twelve miles long. Viewing it from high in the air, the island is shaped like the deck of a huge aircraft carrier. And this, indeed, is a ship that has been buffeted by the winds of change and the seas of scandal.

That the glamorous bloom of Palm Beach is only slightly frayed at the edges is credited to its residents' resilience, wealth, and experience with such matters. In Palm Beach it all has happened before. For this island ship is moored to a rather murky past.

It was ninety-eight years ago that Henry Flagler ran a railroad line down through eastern Florida and built the Royal Poinciana Hotel. He was an enormously wealthy man; along with Stephen Harkness and Henry H. Rogers, he was an original partner of John D. Rockefeller in Standard Oil. When Flagler came to Palm Beach he was well into his sixties and was carrying on with and would later marry a woman forty years his junior, Mary Lily Kenan. Her family still owns The Breakers Hotel. After Flagler died she married Robert Worth Bingham. She died an untimely and mysterious death; however, the money her husband inherited helped start the Louisville *Courier-Journal* and *Louisville Times* newspapers.

If that weren't bad enough, there was Palm Beach's rather raffish resident in the 1920s, one Paris Singer. His father was Isaac Singer, the inventor of the first practical sewing machine, who was in partnership with Edward Clarke. The Clarke fortune, which is still sizable, endured because the family didn't put their trust in money but rather their money in trusts.

The Singer fortune was dissipated within one generation. The problem was Isaac Singer's emotional instability. He had twenty-four children, of whom only six were legitimate. One of the six was Paris Singer, who was known for two things: carrying on a love affair with the dancer Isadora Duncan, and, along with the architect Addison Mizner in the 1920s, changing the face of Palm Beach to Mediterranean Revival—or what some cynics still insist on calling Bull Market Renaissance.

Today, to live in a house designed by Mizner and keep its architectural integrity is considered one of the better social statuses in Palm Beach. Another is membership in the right clubs.

Palm Beach's club life is as circumscribed as its past is murky. The three most important clubs in the town of Palm Beach are the predominantly Jewish Palm Beach Country Club, The Everglades Club, and the B&T, as the Bath & Tennis Club is called. The yearly dues of the latter two respectively run $3500 and $2500—hardly a substantial amount when the price of a house in between the clubs, as the area between The Everglades Club and B&T is referred to, can run up to $14 million. But money isn't the issue. Both clubs are restricted to Gentiles, as they refer to themselves in Palm Beach.

Such a policy has produced a thicket of problems. A female member of the B&T was suspended for six months for inviting a fashion journalist to lunch. One of the thorniest of issues develops when a member becomes either a widow or widower, or divorced, and marries a person of the Jewish faith. The new spouse doesn't become a member, and isn't even allowed on club grounds. While some members who find themselves in this situation of divided loyalties resign, most maintain their club membership and play golf, tennis, or attend club functions without their spouse. The prevailing theory in Palm Beach is that while marriages may

not last, the clubs always will.

Golf has been very much part of the Palm Beach scene since 1897. That year Flagler was building The Royal Poinciana, and also installing a nine-hole golf course. A true workaholic, Flagler viewed golf as a rather frivolous pastime. He once wrote that golf was "a foolish man chasing a silly ball through the woods." He was hardly flushed with pride when he completed the course's little clubhouse, as he refused to install toilets. In 1901, when he was expanding the Palm Beach Inn and changing its name to The Breakers, he added another nine holes, and the Royal Poinciana Country Club became the first eighteen-hole course in Florida.

However, it wasn't until the end of World War I that the first flowering of golf truly began in Palm Beach. It was then establishing itself as a winter playground for society to complement such summer playgrounds as Bar Harbor, Newport, and Tuxedo Park. The Everglades Club was the first club founded in 1919; however, it was a club born of misconception and poor judgment.

In 1918 Paris Singer dreamed up the idea of creating a hospital home for shell-shocked veterans. He hired Mizner to design the building. It was called the Touchstone Convalescent Club. When it was finished in the fall of that year, he sent out thousands of invitations to convalescing officers, but the hospital remained empty. It seemed that none of the veterans wanted to go that far south.

So Singer, hearing the first beats of the Jazz Age, gave away all the expensive hospital equipment, decided to start a club, and gave it the romantic and enticing name of The Everglades Club. With twenty-five charter members, the club officially opened January 25, 1919, and almost immediately became the social center of Palm Beach.

Whether the club made Worth Avenue or the avenue made the club doesn't really matter. What is important is that they exist side-by-side and help give the avenue that special cachet.

Walk west on Worth Avenue, past such famous and fashionable stores as Saks Fifth Avenue, Cartier, Hermes, Gucci, and Brooks Brothers, and on the south side of the street you reach an elegant beige-colored

**ABOVE, TOP.** Playa Riente, the Dodge Estate, was the grandest Mizner mansion in Palm Beach until it was demolished in 1957. **ABOVE.** The mercurial Paris Singer, son of sewing-machine magnate Isaac Singer. **LEFT.** Henry Flagler and his wife, Mary Lily Keman.

**PHOTO PAGE 48.** The 417-yard, par-4 18th hole and the clubhouse at Seminole Golf Club.

52

**ABOVE, TOP.** Addison Mizner's Everglades Club and Yacht Basin.
**ABOVE.** Mrs. Henry C. Phipps powers a drive on the Breakers hotel
course in 1914.

Mediterranean Revival-styled stucco building with white trim, stained-glass windows, and an orange-tiled roof. The only indication that this is a club is a small sign with black and gold letters which reads *Private. Members only.*

Inside to the left are the tennis courts and straight ahead is the golf course. It's a very pleasant course stretching over flattish terrain, measuring only 5655 yards and playing to a par 70. On sixteen of the holes water comes into play. If all the golf course designers who added their touch to the course had been dress designers, The Everglades Club would be one of the chicest stores on Worth Avenue.

The club's first nine holes were designed by Seth Raynor in 1919. Another nine were added in 1928, designed by Donald Ross. In 1937 the architectural team of William Lanford and Theodore Moreau, who had redesigned The Breakers Course in 1926, redesigned it. In the 1960s Mark Mahannah did some work on it, and in the 1970s, new greens were reshaped by George and Tom Fazio.

In 1924 the Gulfstream Golf Club opened in Delray Beach just south of Palm Beach. Its elegant beige stucco clubhouse, which was designed by Mizner, hugs the beach. The golf course, designed by Donald Ross, is located across the road and plays over gently rolling terrain. It measures 6252 yards and plays to a par 71. The course's claim to fame is its 18th hole, measuring 375 yards. It plays right along the beach and over some of the most expensive real estate in Palm Beach, valued at $20,000 per yard.

On January 1, 1930, Palm Beach resident Charles Amory told his young daughter Grace, "We're going to a brand-new club today, so you have to behave yourself." It was the official opening of the Seminole Golf Club ten miles north of Palm Beach in the town of June.

Today Seminole's golf course has ascended into golf's rare stratosphere as one of the greatest courses in the world, along with Muirfield in Scotland, the Old Course; Royal County Down in Northern Ireland; Pebble Beach Golf Links; Augusta National Golf Club; and Royal Melbourne in Australia. (In *Golf Digest*'s latest ranking of great golf courses it's now 14th.) No less an

authority than Ben Hogan, an honorary member, once said, "Seminole is the only course I could be perfectly happy playing every single day. If you can play well there, you can play well anywhere." In the 1950s Hogan used to hone his game there prior to playing in the Masters.

The club is as exclusive as its course is difficult. In the mid-1980s the reigning U.S. Women's Amateur champion was in Palm Beach. For years she had heard glorious reports about Seminole and she desperately wanted to play the course.

One of the unwritten rules at golf and country clubs is that they often extend guest-playing privileges to national champions, Walker and Curtis Cup team members, and prominent male and female professional golfers. The reason is that the club's proud members want their course tested against the game's best, and hope the guests, in turn, will respond with some generous comments about the course such as, "It's the greatest course I've played."

The female champion telephoned Seminole's genial and diplomatic head golf professional, Jerry Pittman. He knew of her and congratulated her on winning the Women's Amateur. The woman then asked if she could play the course. Pittman asked if she knew a member. The woman replied that a woman friend belonged but that she was out of town. She then asked if she could play as Pittman's guest.

"I'll tell you," replied Pittman, "I've been the professional here since 1973 and in all that time I've never had a guest."

Realizing that her request to play had been politely rebuffed the woman replied in a huff, "Well, I suppose Jack Nicklaus can play whenever he wants."

"Mr. Nicklaus," answered Pittman, "plays the allotted guest's privilege of three times a month, and he always plays with a member."

Such is Seminole's prestige that in 1967, when a writer asked Jack Nicklaus what he thought was his greatest disappointment in golf, the writer expected to hear about Nicklaus's failure in defending the U.S. Open championship, or not even making the cut in the 1963 U.S. Open at The Country Club, or playing poorly over the final two holes in the 1963 British Open at Royal

53

54

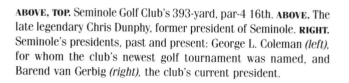

**ABOVE, TOP.** Seminole Golf Club's 393-yard, par-4 16th. **ABOVE.** The late legendary Chris Dunphy, former president of Seminole. **RIGHT.** Seminole's presidents, past and present: George L. Coleman *(left)*, for whom the club's newest golf tournament was named, and Barend van Gerbig *(right)*, the club's current president.

Lytham and St. Annes and losing a playoff bid to Bob Charles and Phil Rogers. But no. "My biggest disappointment," said Nicklaus, "was not getting into Seminole."

Seminole was the dream of Edward F. Hutton, founder of the brokerage firm, and Martin Sweeney. Hutton was unable to crack the waiting list at Gulf-stream Golf Club and so decided to start his own club. At the time he was the second husband of Marjorie Merriweather Post. Marion Wyeth, the architect who designed their grand home, Mar-a-Largo, designed the salmon-pink stucco Mediterranean-styled clubhouse at Seminole.

The clubhouse reflects what matters most at Seminole: golf. It's a small, elegant building with thick mahogany doors and a red-tiled roof. Both the dining room and the main living room are small, with windows overlooking the sand dunes and the ocean. There's a swimming pool, but it hardly ever gets used. Nowhere is the mood of the club better reflected than in the men's locker room.

It's a spacious, airy room with fireplaces at either end, a high-beamed ceiling, built-in cedar lockers and thirteen mounted animal heads staring down at half a dozen overstuffed sofas, a dozen lounging chairs, a bar, and a long table that is covered in the afternoons with cheese and crackers and several jars of a Seminole tradition: ginger snaps.

There are no nameplates on the lockers. One reason given is that each of the 325 members knows where his locker is. But, of course, the real reason is that the club's Board of Governors does not want guests to know who the members are, most of whom either winter in Palm Beach or Hobe Sound and spend the majority of the rest of the year on Long Island's North Shore, Southampton, or Greenwich, Connecticut.

Most members also claim that Seminole and not Pinehurst No. 2 is Donald Ross's best-designed course. In the spring of 1928 Ross was hired by Hutton and Sweeney. For two weeks he went up and down the coastline north and south of Palm Beach. He finally found 174 acres, but to the dismay of the members, the land was ten miles north of Palm Beach. What he envisioned is like dreaming in color.

Ross found an almost perfect square parcel of oceanfront land protected by a high escarpment; as the years rolled by this would prove to be important. The land sloped downward into a huge mangrove swamp and then moved upward to sixty-five feet above sea level.

During the summer of 1928 and into the fall, a work force that Ross brought down from Pinehurst, with two steamshovels hauled by mules, drained the mangrove swamp so construction could begin to shape the fairways. If Seminole isn't Ross's best work, it's unequivocally his best-routed course. To take the fullest advantage of the wind (which in February, March, and April is predominantly a southeast wind), the elevation, and the coastline, Ross designed each nine going in different directions. The outgoing nine run somewhat counterclockwise and the incoming nine, clockwise.

The best golf hole played along the high ground is the 390-yard, par-4 6th. Tommy Armour once said it was "the finest single golf hole in the United States."

From the tee the hole swings slightly left. The drive must clear a yawning bunker down the left side. A drive hit too far down the left side will catch one of three more bunkers. Depending on the wind, a perfect drive in the fairway can leave anything from a four-iron to a nine-iron shot; however, the approach shot to the green must clear four bunkers that are pushed diagonally across the fairway, guarding the green set on the bias of the fairway.

It would be difficult to find three more exciting finishing holes in America, in which no water comes into play, than the final three at Seminole. They consist of two medium-length par-4 holes sandwiching a medium-length par-3. When a southeast wind is sweeping in off the Atlantic, they provide a very testy finish. The 16th is a dogleg right of 393 yards. The drive is downwind, but where the fairway swings right, there are a total of ten sand bunkers lining the fairway to the green. The second short is slightly uphill and played into a crosswind. The 175-yard, par-3 17th runs along the top of the escarpment. The hole usually plays directly into the wind. Any tee shot hit with a high howling hook will send the ball out of bounds and onto the beach. Guarding the green are five bunkers. The 417-yard 18th is a dogleg left. The

55

tee is perched above the fairway on the escarpment. The drive must clear a huge bunker on the left side of the fairway. The second shot is all uphill to a green that hugs the beach, and it is guarded by two deep bunkers right of the green and one left, beyond which is out of bounds.

The 18th hole is the only major change the course has undergone. Originally, the 18th was a fairly easy straightaway par-4. The tee was situated below and right of the 17th green, and the 18th green, which is now the practice pitch-and-putt green, was below the escarpment and level with the fairway. The reason for such an easy and high stroke hole was then Ross's architectural philosophy. He didn't believe that a match between two average golfers should be determined on a stroke hole.

In 1947 Dick Wilson was hired to redesign the 18th. It was kept a secret for almost forty years. The decision to hire Wilson was made by the guiding spirit of the club from just after World War II, for over thirty years the often charming and irascible Christopher Dunphy. Once when Hogan complained about the greens being too slow Dunphy retorted, "If you didn't take so much time to putt the grass wouldn't get that long."

He was what every club needs, a man of financial means who has taken early retirement and found his life's purpose in the club. He arranged matches, was a genial host and, along with the green superintendent, T. Claiborn Watson, made Seminole a very exciting place to golf. They set about restoring the course after World War II to its former glory and even beyond. For the winter the fairways were planted with Ormond Bermuda grass so the ball sits up beautifully and the greens were seeded with the finest Tiftdwarf Bermuda; the greens are kept firm and range from 9 to 11 on the stemmeter.

After World War II, golf again began to blossom in Palm Beach. In 1947 Wilson designed the West Palm Beach Country Club, which still today is ranked as one of the best daily-fee courses in America.

The course is built on a duneline a mile south of the Palm Beach International Airport. With its wonderful use of elevation and treelined fairways, it resembles a northeastern course. As the course matured, it became so good that from 1954 to 1962 it was host to the West Palm Beach Open, a regular stop on the PGA Tour. The winner in 1959 was Arnold Palmer.

The course gets heavy play—almost 95,000 rounds annually. And in these days of escalating green fees, some as much as $100, at West Palm Beach Country Club they are kept down to a very reasonable $22 for a resident. A golf cart priced at $9 is mandatory but only up until 1 P.M.; then the golfer can walk.

All this is possible because when the property was deeded to the City of West Palm Beach by several philanthropists, they were decades ahead of their time. They stipulated that the course would be operated as a municipal course by an independent golf commission of five West Palm Beach business and professional residents. By removing the golf course from the hands of the local politicians and privatizing it, they could offer very reasonable golf, employ more than fifty people, and even pay the City of West Palm Beach a nice annual sum of money.

Wilson also designed the Palm Beach Par 3 Golf Course in Lake Worth. This is one of the best and most exciting par-3 courses in the country. Covering forty-two acres and measuring 2600 yards, the course is bordered on one side by the Atlantic Ocean and the other by the Intercoastal Waterway. Four holes, the 4th through the 7th, cover almost 1700 feet and play along the Atlantic; three holes, the 11th through the 13th, run almost 1400 feet and play along the Waterway. Not only is the course an ideal place for beginners to learn golf, but for those golfers who understand that mastering the short game is the essence of good scoring, this is the perfect place to hone their short game. Annually the course gets over 55,000 rounds, with green fees for the winter at $15.50 and $8 in the summer.

The success of the Par 3 is a story of Palm Beach at its best. When the citizens get together for a common cause, they can be a mighty force. The course originally was built by Ogden Phipps in 1960. In 1971 he decided to sell; instead of selling the land to developers he suggested the Town of Palm Beach buy it. The town's citizens voted for it and the town bought the course for $15 million. Later the residents had the great foresight to designate the land as a greenbelt, which could only be used as a golf course, so that future generations of

56

**ABOVE.** The dangerous green of the 175-yard, par-3 17th hole at Seminole. **LEFT.** Palm Beach's own Robin Weiss, 1989 Women's Mid-Amateur Champion.

**OVERLEAF.** The Gulf Stream Golf Club. Its 18th hole along the ocean occupies some of the most expensive real estate in Palm Beach County.

Palm Beachers would have a place to play golf.

Besides the Par 3, The Everglades Club, and The Breakers Hotel Course, the other course that makes up the quartet of courses in the Town of Palm Beach is The Palm Beach Country Club. It's located two miles north of The Breakers Hotel on North Ocean Boulevard. Although the course dates back to the 1920s and was originally designed by Donald Ross, it has had a variety of owners and names. The present club was founded in 1953. It sits on eighty-eight acres bordered on the east by the Atlantic Ocean and protected on three sides by tall hedges and a high fence.

Three years ago the 300-plus members had a brand-new, two-story, Mediterranean-style clubhouse built. Its large front windows face the Atlantic; a terrace on the west side faces the golf course. Unlike so many courses in south Florida that are flat, Palm Beach's is almost hilly. Beneath much of the course runs an underground coral reef that long ago was covered with sand, dirt, and grass, so that two-thirds of the golf holes play over hills and down dales. In 1989 the course was stretched from 5771 to 6200 yards and two long par-4's were converted to par-5's, and the par was increased from 68 to 70.

While it's often said that playing the famed course at the Pine Tree Golf Club from the championship tees is a way of separating the men from the boys, golf at Palm Beach Country Club may be said to separate the golfer from his money. Not only is the club one of the hardest to get into, its initiation fee is $80,000 and its annual dues $3500. One must not only have money to get in, but must always be willing to give it away. "Charity," said one of the club's former presidents, "is a must."

While the 1920s witnessed the first generation of golfers in Palm Beach, the 1950s to mid-1960s welcomed the second generation. The time was shaped by the golf course architects Dick Wilson and the team of George and Tom Fazio, and four real estate developers: John Dodge, Llwyd Ecclestone Sr., John D. MacArthur, and Arthur Vinning Davis.

Besides designing the West Palm Beach Country Club and the Par 3, Wilson also designed the Pine Tree Golf Club in Boynton Beach (site of the 1978 Senior Amateur) and the East Course at the JDM Country Club in Palm Beach Gardens. George Fazio designed one of Florida's best courses, the Hills Course at Jupiter Hills Country Club. As so many new courses are born out of dissatisfaction with other courses, this course was born out of dissatisfaction with the weather. Fazio and William Clay Ford were playing in the Bing Crosby Pro-Am in Pebble Beach in the late 1960s. It was—as is often referred to as typical Crosby weather—cold, rainy, and windy. Ford asked Fazio if he could find a sunny place to play golf. Fazio found 366 acres in Jupiter, Florida, straddling Palm Beach and Martin Counties. Bob Hope and Philadelphian William Elliott formed the club, and over its hilly terrain Fazio designed a magnificent course. It was the site of the 1987 U.S. Amateur.

Among the developers responsible for turning Florida into a golfer's mecca during this time were John Dodge, who in the 1950s developed the Country Club of Florida and later Quail Ridge Country Club, and developer Llwyd Ecclestone Sr., who in 1960 founded Lost Tree Country Club in North Palm Beach.

However, their legacies pale beside those of MacArthur and Davis. Near the end of his life MacArthur owned 100,000 acres of land in Florida, which made him the state's largest landowner. He was responsible not only for creating JDM Country Club and Frenchman's Creek Country Club but also for developing entire towns, including Palm Beach Gardens and North Palm Beach. (MacArthur's foundation, set up after his death and known for its "genius awards," is now one of the five largest foundations in the country.)

In 1956 Arthur Vinning Davis, cofounder of the Aluminum Corporation of America (Alcoa) bought the Boca Raton Hotel and Club and 1500 surrounding acres; later through his Arvida real estate company he established Boca West and Broken Sound developments.

The third generation of Palm Beach golfers arrived in the 1980s as developers pushed northward and westward, and more than twenty new golf courses were completed. Two clubs aged and matured to such a high level that they were chosen to host national championships this past fall: the Loxahatchee Club was the site of the Senior Amateur and Old Marsh Golf Club was the site of the Women's Mid-Amateur.

62

**ABOVE.** Teeing off at the 466-yard, par-4 15th hole at Old Marsh, site of the Women's Mid-Amateur. **RIGHT.** Florida's leading conservationist, Nathaniel Reed, at Old Marsh.

**PRECEDING PAGE.** The difficult 190-yard, par-3 9th at Jupiter Hills Club.

Loxahatchee was another dream course of another very wealthy man and avid golfer, Gordon Gray, chairman of Royal LePage of Canada. The course is the center of a 320-acre development dotted with blue ponds and tall pines. Gray hired his friend and occasional fishing companion, Jack Nicklaus, to design the course. On what had been a flat and featureless land, Nicklaus built huge, grassy "chocolate-drop mounds" and moguls covered with lovegrass that separate the fairways and frame the target area, giving the course the look of an old British seaside course.

Soon the club began to attract golfers from such prestigious northeastern clubs as National Golf Links of America, Shinnecock Hills Golf Club, and The Rockaway Hunting Club, whose members liked their golf played over windswept courses near the sea. They also liked the fact that the course has year-round bent-grass greens. They're large and undulating, and in the winter when it's neither too hot nor too humid, the greens can be cut very short, and become very fast.

Six miles southeast of Loxahatchee is Old Marsh Golf Club in Palm Beach Gardens. Open since 1987, the club spreads over 450 acres and, like Loxahatchee, membership is limited to around 300.

Old Marsh is a triumph. Built around a secluded fragile marshland, the course was carefully designed with ecological concerns in mind—a situation that will be increasingly common in south Florida if development is to continue, as less and less prime land becomes available. Much of the credit for promoting the awareness of such ecological concerns in the area is due to Nathaniel Reed, a former Assistant Secretary of the Interior. He's the state's leading conservationist and has helped the South Florida Water Management District protect the region's water and aquatic vegetation by setting stringent requirements for developers. "Old Marsh is an environmental masterpiece," says Reed. "From now on any builder who wants to build a course near a marsh will have to look at it carefully."

The course was designed by Pete Dye. "Because of the South Florida Water Management District I designed a better course," says Dye. All the fairways slope slightly inward, as all the drainage is in the middle of the course rather than at the outer edges of the fairway.

63

OVERLEAF. The 5th hole at Old Marsh Golf Club.

66

**ABOVE.** At the PGA National Golf Club, the 18th green of the 567-yard, par-5 of the General Course. **RIGHT.** The designing family. Golf course architect Pete Dye *(center),* his son P.B. *(left),* and his wife Alice *(right)* at the Cypress Course designed by Pete and P.B.—the Palm Beach Polo and Country Club.

Dye incorporated the marshlands and the lakes so effectively that on every hole one or the other comes into play. The result is a wonderful variety of golf holes that constantly test and tease the golfer. There are drives over marshlands and blind pitch shots over mounds. On those days when a stiff wind is sweeping across the course, man can direct the ball, but only providence can determine its fate.

Five miles northwest of Old Marsh in Palm Beach Gardens is the PGA National Golf Club, also founded by Ecclestone. The 2340-acre property, which also boasts some 3000 private homes and a 335-room hotel, is the home of the Professional Golfers Association of America, the backbone of professional golf; the United States Croquet Association; and four golf courses: The Haig, named after Walter Hagen; The Squire, named after Gene Sarazen; The General, named after Arnold Palmer, who designed it with Ed Seay; and The Champion.

The Champion is the best course. Along with The Haig and The Squire, The Champion originally was designed by Tom and George Fazio and opened in 1981. In 1983 it was the site of the Ryder Cup Matches, and in 1987, it hosted the PGA championship, won by Larry Nelson. Since 1983 it has been the site of the PGA Seniors championship. In 1989 the course was redesigned by Jack Nicklaus.

Eleven miles west of Palm Beach, across the Waterway, past the town of West Palm Beach and six miles southwest of Palm Beach International Airport, where the roads run flat and hopes soar high, is The Palm Beach Polo and Country Club, a 2200-acre resort community. It has had two identities. The first was established by William Ylvisaker, chairman of the board of Gould Electronics in Chicago. He, along with Paul Butler, helped establish Oak Brook, Illinois, as one of America's polo capitals. Since the passing away of George Sherman and polo at the Gulfstream Club in the early 1970s there had been little polo played around Palm Beach; Ylvisaker wanted to revive interest in polo and in 1978 he created Palm Beach Polo and Country Club.

He did more than just revive interest in polo—he made the club the winter capital for high-goal polo in America and the winter headquarters of international polo. From December through April, weekends there are now filled with polo matches; spectators come out to watch polo, to sip champagne, and to look at other people's Rolex watches.

Ylvisaker also brought good golf to the community. He hired George and Tom Fazio to design the original course, of which only nine holes remain. (It's unimaginatively named the Old Course.) He then hired a former U.S. Amateur and Open champion, Jerry Pate, and architect Ron Garl to design the Dunes Course, which opened in November 1985.

In October of 1986 Gould Electronics sold the community to Landmark Land for $40 million. (Palm Beach Polo and Country Club and all of Landmark Land properties now are in Chapter 11.) While many famous people have resided at the club, its most famous, when not on the PGA Tour, is the enormously talented star of the 1991 Ryder Cup Matches and winner of the 1992 Masters, America's new golfing hero, Fred Couples. In a sport that weekly puts out enough media hype to fill the deepest bunker, Couples' shy and genuine manner is as refreshing as the morning dew on the first green.

The club's Cypress Course, designed by Pete Dye and his son, P.B. Dye, opened in October 1988. It features pot bunkers, railroad ties, and even a par-4 with old-fashioned cross-fairway bunkering. The course's signature hole is the par-5, 641-yard (520 for members) 17th, where water runs all the way down the left side of the fairway. Says P.B. Dye, "We wanted to design a par-five where Fred Couples couldn't reach the green in two shots."

Through times of change and times of scandal golf has flourished in Palm Beach for almost a century. Here the game's future exceeds its grasp. "I think," says P.B. Dye wryly, "developers are going to run out of land on which to build courses before they run out of golfers to sell it to."

67

# PALM SPRINGS

**P**alm Springs lies 107 miles southeast of Los Angeles in the Colorado Desert in what the residents quaintly call The Valley, but what is properly known as the Coachella Valley; it begins in the Valley's westernmost city of Palm Springs and stretches eastward thirty miles to Indio. It is an inspiring place of contrast and change. For no matter how many winters you winter there, or how many weekends you weekend there, you are always awed by the rawness of the land. Thrusting upward more than 10,000 feet from the desert floor are the bare, rocky San Jacinto Mountains, their peaks capped with snow during the winter. Ugly networks of wind-seared ridges weave to the desert floor. A whining wind blows down them and out in the open spaces send tumbleweeds drifting across the desert. Most of this desert, with its gouged-out washes, is barren except for cacti, sagebrush mesquite, and rattlesnakes. This is not the good earth, it seems.

But to walk now in parts of the Valley, that for so long was considered barren and fruitless, and smell the orange blossoms, is to know the wonders born of the desert. There are thousands of orange and grapefruit trees, willows, cedars, and olive trees—all transplanted, thriving and looking as if, like the fig trees, they have always been there. Fairways glisten bright green next to the parched, beige earth.

This is the home of America's wealthiest Native American tribe, the Agua Caliente, a former President of the United States, Gerald R. Ford, and a former Ambassador to the Court of St. James, Walter H. Annenberg. It's also the home of one hundred golf courses and the winter home of thousands of semi-retired or retired corporate executives and dozens of active and retired movie stars with streets named after them: Bob Hope Drive, Frank Sinatra Drive, Gene Autry Drive, and Dinah Shore Drive.

In contrast to the glitter and glamour, The Valley is also home to the hope of lives to be regenerated, at one of the world's finest sites for drug and alcohol rehabilitation—the Betty Ford Center.

70

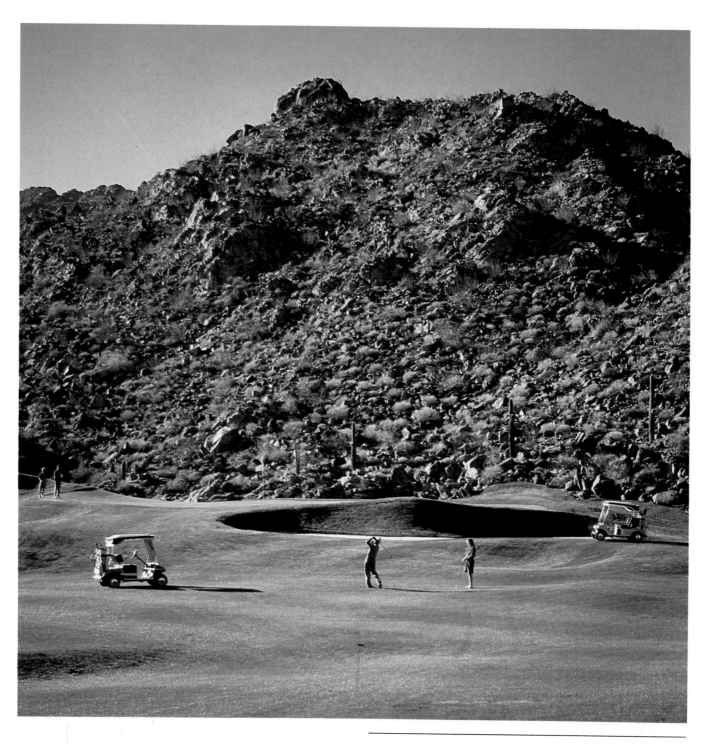

The No. 1 green at Bighorn.

PHOTO PAGE 68. The 17th hole at PGA West.

The Valley is also the place of choice of thousands of people who decided to live there permanently, to work and raise families. What is it like growing up in Palm Springs? Said one woman, who grew up there and later graduated from Stanford University, "Being raised in Palm Springs is like growing up in a land of movie stars and in a place where the leaves don't change color."

The first visitors began passing through Palm Springs as early as 1853, when a government survey party mapped Palm Springs and established the first wagon route through the San Gorgonio Pass. In 1877, as an incentive to complete the railroad line to the Pacific, the government offered the Southern Pacific Railroad odd-numbered sections of land for ten miles on each side of the tracks through the Southern California Desert. The Agua Calientes were given the even-numbered sections of land, though by federal law they were forbidden to sell or lease their land or gain any income from it. The conditions of the Indians were reported to the Congress of the United States in 1883: "There is in this desert a reservation called Agua Caliente, of about 60,000 acres. From the best information we can get, this is all barren, desert land with only one spring in it. These desert Indians are wretchedly poor, and need help perhaps more than any other in Southern California." Through the decades, bitter court battles raged concerning the Indians' right to the land. Finally in 1944 the Supreme Court of the United States gave the Agua Calientes legal right to have allotments approved. But over the years bureaucratic red tape held up the process. In 1959 President Dwight D. Eisenhower signed the Equalization Law allowing the Agua Calientes the legal right to sell and to lease their land for profit. Today, the Agua Caliente are the largest landowners in the City of Palm Springs with nearly 6700 of their 32,500 acres within the city limits. An acre of land in the center of Palm Springs can run up to $3 million.

In 1931 Palm Springs had one paved road and two hotels. But it was the sunshine that actor Charles Farrell wanted. "I was worn out from pictures," said the star of *Seventh Heaven*. "I just wanted to sit in the sun and play a little tennis." With his friend, actor Ralph Bellamy, he bought 200 acres in Palm Springs for $30 per acre and founded the Racquet Club. And soon Palm Springs became a favorite place for some of Hollywood's stars to play tennis—and to carry on romantic trysts.

When wealthy oil man Thomas O'Donnell built the first nine-hole golf course in Palm Springs in 1928, he also bought 750 shares of the Whitewater Mutual Water Company and piped water in from the White Water Canyon fourteen miles away to irrigate his course.

Twenty-two years elapsed before Palm Springs got its first eighteen-hole golf course. The man responsible and the father of golf in Palm Springs was Johnny Dawson. He was a man with a combination of rare and distinct talents. He was a highly visual person, a visionary, an astute salesman, and a champion golfer. He was born in 1902 and raised in Wheaton, Illinois, outside of Chicago. His father was an Australian who worked for the Rand-McNally Map Company. Johnny was the second son in a family of five brothers and one sister. Like so many outstanding golfers of the time, Dawson learned about golf as a caddie. When he was eleven years old he began caddying at the Green Valley Golf Course. As he grew older he became a fine athlete and was good enough to play end on the Wheaton High School football team. He blocked for his halfback, who would become one of the game's all-time great runners—Red Grange.

At first Dawson wanted to be a commercial artist and he spent two years studying at the Chicago Art Institute. At age twenty-four he burst upon the amateur golf scene when he reached the semi-finals of the 1926 U.S. Amateur at the Baltusrol Golf Club. In 1928 he got to the third round. His peak years seemed just ahead of him, and there was surely a strong possibility of victory in a national championship. But in 1929 the United States Golf Association declared Dawson a nonamateur because he was a salesman for A.G. Spalding & Company, and he wasn't allowed to compete in the amateur championship sponsored by the USGA. However, he could compete in other open and amateur competitions. In 1930 he won the Houston Open and in 1936 the prestigious Trans-Mississippi Amateur. Then in 1942 he pulled off something of a California slam by winning the California Open and Amateur and the

Southern California Amateur. He would go on to win the Southern California Amateur in 1944, 1945, and 1952. During World War II he sold real estate in Southern California, and after the war he regained his full amateur status. In 1947 he lost in the final of the U.S. Amateur to Robert (Skee) Riegal, 2 and 1. He was selected to the 1949 U.S. team for the Walker Cup Matches to be played at the Winged Foot Golf Club. In foursomes, he and Bruce McCormick won 8 and 7, and in singles he beat Joe Carr 5 and 3.

During these years Dawson was making frequent trips to the Coachella Valley. He realized golf would flourish in the desert, but six factors had to be considered: water, soil, sun, view, wind, and washes. He had the soil analyzed and discovered that, by adding the right mixture of sulphur and certain fertilizers, it could become very fertile. Next came the sun and water. It has been said that what oil is to Texas, sun is to Palm Springs. This is more the tissue than the bone of truth. As Dawson said, "The most vital element isn't sun, it's water. If you didn't have water you wouldn't have anything. People love the sun, but they love gazing at greenery."

Though the average rainfall in the Coachella Valley is less than twelve inches annually, if it didn't rain for the next hundred years it wouldn't matter. Just north of the Palm Springs city limits, running into the town of Indio, is a twenty-mile-long underground water basin. Over the last 32 years 2000 wells have been drilled. Each well is capable of producing over one million gallons of water daily. How much water is in the basin? One estimate states that there is enough water to serve two million people for two million years.

After taking several flights over the desert, Dawson noticed deep paths in the sand caused by wind and water rushing off the mountains. Such areas would be unsuitable for growing grass. Then, with watch in hand, he found that east of the San Jacinto Mountains he would gain thirty minutes more of sunlight in the winter.

This brought him to the Thunderbird Dude Ranch, a 663-acre spread ten miles east of Palm Springs. It offered an excellent view of the Santa Rosa Mountains, but more important, it has an artesian well capable of producing 2000 gallons of water a minute.

The ranch was owned by Frank Bogert. He had named it for the mythical and sacred Indian Thunderbird known for creating lightning and thunder with the flap of his wings. This, and an additional eighty acres adjoining the ranch, was acquired.

Potential investors, however, seeing the desolate land of sand and brush and a ranch house with no glass windows, thought Dawson's brain had been addled by too much sun. When he took the current U.S. Open champion, Ben Hogan, to the site, Hogan said, "You'll never build a golf course out here."

But, Hogan was never a speculator. Oilmen are. One of them invested $100,000 in the yet-unnamed project, and soon a contingent from Hollywood joined in: Bing Crosby, Bob Hope, Phil Harris. Baseball great Ralph Kiner joined them. Lawrence M. Hughes, who had been a construction supervisor for golf course architect Donald Ross before World War II, and who had designed the Mission Valley Country Club course (now the Stardust Country Club) in San Diego, was hired as the architect. "Building the course was just a question of pushing sand around," said Dawson.

Many people who were lucky enough to possess a vision of the future bought lots along the golf course for $2000 each. The course officially opened in the fall of 1951. Within a year half of the eighty-seven lots were sold. More of Hollywood followed: Lucille Ball and Desi Arnaz, Hoagy Carmichael, Randolph Scott, and June Allyson. Ernest Breech Jr., a member of the club and chairman of the Ford Motor Company, was so enamored of the sporty and high-toned atmosphere of the club that he decided to name the company's newest sports car the Thunderbird, after the club. The first car was given to Johnny Dawson.

In 1955 the Ryder Cup Matches were played at Thunderbird. The U.S. team beat the team from Great Britain and Ireland 8 and 4. In 1959 the Ryder Cup again returned to The Valley, this time to the Eldorado Country Club. And again the results were almost as predictable with the U.S. team winning 8½ to 3½.

Two years after Thunderbird opened, Tamarisk Country Club opened just down the road and immediately became famous because of two men. Its pro was the great Ben Hogan, and the club proved it was right

**ABOVE.** Johnny Dawson, the father of golf in Palm Springs, with his wife, Velma. The Thunderbird car was named for the Thunderbird Country Club, the first country club founded in the Coachella Valley. **LEFT.** Lucille Ball and Desi Arnaz, early members of Thunderbird.

**ABOVE.** The 3rd hole of La Quinta's Citrus Course. **LEFT.** The 15th hole at Thunderbird.

and one man was wrong—a man who once said, "I wouldn't want to belong to any club that would accept me as a member." Groucho Marx became a very happy club member. Then Indian Wells Country Club opened. A golf boom was on in The Valley. The United States had a golfing president in Dwight Eisenhower, and a new golfing hero in Arnold Palmer, a man who kept hitching up his trousers, smoking cigarettes, and willing in putts. In 1959 La Quinta Country Club opened ceremoniously with President Eisenhower cutting the ribbon and hitting the first drive.

In 1961 The Valley witnessed the building of the last of the great estate golf courses in the United States. The owner was Walter H. Annenberg, a keen golfer whose interest in the game goes back to the 1920s when, as a boy, he caddied for the great Bobby Jones at the Lakeville Course in Great Neck, Long Island. A visionary genius, Annenberg purchased 250 acres on what is now just off Frank Sinatra Drive. He was following a grand tradition of enormously wealthy men who loved golf and liked to see trees grow on money.

Just before the turn of the century John D. Rockefeller built a four-hole golf course on his estate in Pocantico Hills, New York. In the 1920s T. Suffern Tailer Sr. built the splendid nine-hole course called The Ocean Links in Newport. In 1929 Henry Francis du Pont, a great grandson of E.I. du Pont, built a nine-hole course at his Winterthur estate. And in the 1950s in Pawling, New York, Lowell Thomas built a nine-hole course and called it Hammerale Hills and Hunt Club.

Annenberg hired Dick Wilson to design his grand course. It has nine large, undulating greens and three different sets of tees. Each nine measures approximately 3000 yards, or 6000 yards for eighteen holes. (From the front tees the course measures 5669 yards.) Uniquely, each set of tees is placed at a different angle to the green, offering a wonderful variety of differently designed golf holes. A certain hole may be a par 4 on the outgoing nine and a par 3 on the incoming nine. Groomed to perfection, the course has bent-grass greens and Bermuda grass fairways. Every September the course is overseeded with Rye grass. Annenberg brought in more than 875 olive trees and installed a

LEFT, TOP. The 1955 U.S. Ryder Cup team at the Thunderbird Club. *(Left to right):* Jerry Barber, Tommy Bolt, Dr. Cary Middlecoff, Doug Ford, Marty Furgol, Chick Harbert, Lloyd Mangrum, Ted Kroll, Sam Snead, Jack Burke Jr., and Chandler Harper. The U.S. team won 8 to 4. LEFT, BOTTOM. Truly a green oasis: Sunnylands II, the estate and golf course of Walter H. Annenberg.

78

ABOVE. The 11th hole at the Vintage Club Mountain Course. RIGHT. President Gerald Ford with Mr. and Mrs. Mick Humphries at a 1984 Vintage Club party.

OVERLEAF. Jack Nicklaus Resort Course, PGA West.

variety of eucalyptus, Virginia oaks, and stone pines.

Here and there on the course, near a tee or at a turn of a dogleg, Annenberg's love of art and art objects is visible. Beyond the third tee is a Chinese teahouse. At the elbow of the dogleg of the 441-yard 5th hole is a totem pole. Reflecting Annenberg's rich sense of humor, he named all the golf holes. A par 3 is called "Sitting Pretty." Another par 3 is named "Baby Baby." The 10th is called "Elegantisima" and the 15th "Indulgence."

Every month during the winter Annenberg gets more than fifty letters from well-meaning golfers who want to play his course. Most of the letters go unanswered. "The course," says Annenberg, "is for myself, my wife and friends. It's by invitation only."

The lucky invitee arrives at a guarded gate. The guard, who has been informed of your arrival, lets you in and then quickly closes the huge iron gate. You drive up a winding driveway lined with olive and palm trees and around back of the mansion with its 32,000 square feet of living space. An attendant escorts you to the locker room. The men's locker room is small and unpretentious. A small sign reads GOLF SPOKEN HERE.

Shoes changed, you are led to the practice tee. There's a pyramid of brand-new golf balls for practice. Annenberg is there and in a cheery voice says, "Welcome to Sunnylands." (This actually is Sunnylands II. The original Sunnylands was the name of Annenberg's father's estate in Milford, Pennsylvania.) On the way to the first tee Annenberg explains the procedure of play. "Guests always have the honor on every tee no matter who had the lowest score on the last hole. The order remains the same through the round. Don't replace divots. A man will come along later with a mixture of seed and fertilizer to repair all divots."

Nobody has ever scored a hole-in-one at Sunnylands. What would be the prize for such a feat? "A bottle of beer," says Annenberg jokingly. Now eighty-six years old, Annenberg sill plays a little—though he is reluctant to reveal his handicap. He was a very strong 18. And he never gambles on the golf course—not even a dollar. He's fond of quoting the late Ed Sullivan who said, "Golf is a game of ease. Not an easy game."

Easy or not, Annenberg helped to popularize golf in The Valley. Then in the early 1960s former President Eisenhower had a winter home built along the 11th airway of Eldorado Country Club. "Ike made Eldorado," says a member. There's even a nearby mountaintop named "Ike's Peak." And all the while, Johnny Dawson kept spreading the word—"There's no finer climate for winter golf than Palm Springs."

But it was Bob Hope who perhaps did more than anyone else to bring national attention to golf in The Valley. In 1960 he inaugurated the Bob Hope Classic (now named the Bob Hope Chrysler Classic). It's the only 90-hole tournament on the PGA Tour and the only tournament played over four courses (one course is used twice) and in which the pro-am part of the tournament lasts four days. Helping to popularize the tournament was the fact that the very first one was won by Arnold Palmer. He won it a total of five times, and his last victory on the PGA tour was the 1973 Hope.

The Valley is one of the few places in the United States that supports a tournament from all three tours. There's the Hope on the PGA Tour. And since 1981 (though not sanctioned by the Senior PGA Tour until 1984), the Vintage Invitational, and one of the four majors of the Ladies' Professional Golf Association, the Nabisco Dinah Shore, is played at the Mission Hills Country Club. Since 1987 the Skins Game was played over the Stadium Course at PGA West. This year it's being played at Big Horn Golf Club. The only national championship ever played in The Valley was the 1985 Mid-Amateur played at The Vintage Club.

While Palm Springs lacks the grand golfing tradition of both Pebble Beach and the Carolina Sandhills, it counters with a quantity of golf courses and a large and enthusiastic golfing population that wants to see the game spread triumphantly across the desert. Success is the only thing they have known. In the 1960s they ousted the polo crowd. (But they returned again to the Eldorado Country Club in the early 1980s.) Then came the tennis boom, and the golfers—always a plucky lot—prevailed. Although there are as many tennis facilities as golf courses in The Valley, the golfing population outnumbers the tennis population by at least a third. During the 1960s and 1970s The Valley's three most prominent clubs were Eldorado, Tamarisk, and Thunderbird. "Those members," said a member,

79

"not only have all the money in The Valley, they have all the money in the world."

All that changed in 1981 with the opening of The Vintage Club in Indian Wells. It drew some members from next-door neighbor Eldorado Country Club, some from Thunderbird, and a few from Tamarisk. Spread over 715 acres, the entire place exudes luxury at every dogleg. The entrance to the club is a wide boulevard lined with tall royal palm trees. Nothing was spared in building the place—not space, not views, and not water. Indeed, water is used so lavishly throughout the property in ponds and lakes, one wonders if Esther Williams was the consultant to the landscape architect. The clubhouse makes a statement of unabashed elegance. The modern structure bears no resemblance to the country-manor style so popular during most of this century for clubhouses. The clubhouse's striking rooflines—a harmony of small pyramids topping pillared wings—play with the desert light and shadows to counterpoint the rippled foothills beyond. Within, floor-to-ceiling glass walls lend light and airiness. But the building's most stunning effect is achieved with water: set within five acres of lakes, the clubhouse literally seems to float. At night, when its golden lights are reflected on the water, it looks like some futuristic seaplane about to take wing.

While the clubhouse is the nerve center of the club, the golf courses are the club's arteries. For one of the club's main attractions is that it offers two 18-hole courses. Both the Desert and Mountain Courses were designed by Tom Fazio. The Desert is the shorter and subtler of the two, measuring just 6271 yards and playing to a par 72. It has a more natural look to it, and actually plays through the raw desert among windflowers and cacti. The Mountain Course measures 6907 yards and also plays to a par 72; it has the majestic Santa Rosa Mountains as a backdrop, which daily change color from purple to charcoal and produce a vivid contrast to the green fairways. The course actually is a meadowland course, gently rolling with tree-lined fairways and ponds. The course's signature hole is the famous par-4, 406-yard 16th. The tee shot must cross a blue pond diagonally to reach the fairway. The closer you want it to get to the green, the more water you have to cross. The par-3, 156-yard 17th requires another per-

fectly gauged tee shot. The green is three-tiered and protected in front and rear by sand bunkers and on the right by water. Not only is there the specter of three-putting, but when the pin is tucked on the lower right, of actually putting off the green into the water.

During the 1960s scores of other courses opened. Jack Nicklaus's first designed course in The Valley was at The Club at Morningside, next door to the Thunderbird Country Club. The club's 18th hole may be the best finishing hole in The Valley. And certainly it's a better finishing hole than Nicklaus's 18th at Muirfield Village Golf Club in Dublin, Ohio. Morningside's 18th measures 559 yards. Two hundred yards from the tee there's water all the way down the right side of the fairway. The green is huge; in fact, it's a double green that's shared with the par-3 12th hole. The green is guarded in front by water, then a sand bunker, and two more sand bunkers behind the green. The green can be hit with two mighty shots; however, the ball must be struck perfectly, as it must carry over the water and the sand, then land softly and hold the green. It's just the kind of shot Nicklaus plays so well.

The most ambitious project in The Valley during the 1980s was PGA West, located in La Quinta. Situated on 2500 acres, it's planned to have eight golf courses (with three open to the public), a 1000-room hotel, and sixty tennis courts. To date, four of the courses have been built, including an Arnold Palmer-designed course, two Jack Nicklaus-designed courses.

When the TPC Stadium course opened at PGA West in January 1986, it was the most notorious new course not only in the Coachella Valley but in the United States. Ernest O. Vossler and Joe W. Walmer, officers of Landmark Land Company, Inc., hired Pete Dye and told him to design the most difficult course in the world. Dye should have known better.

Over what had been a celery field, Dye had millions of cubic feet of earth moved to create lakes and streams, cavernous sand bunkers, and fairways that twist and turn every which way and are filled with moguls and hollows. The end result was a golf course so demanding, so severe, so penalizing, and so unfair that it's playable to any degree of effectiveness only by a small fraction of the golfing population. Unlike Pine-

83

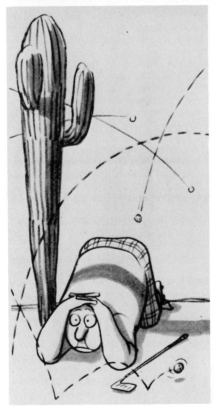

**ABOVE, TOP.** The Lakes Country Club. **ABOVE.** The 18th hole at Bermuda Dunes, with the clubhouse in the background.

The 16th hole at Vintage Club.

hurst No. 2, it completely lacks the scent of golf. And making matters worse, every golf hole was given a name suggestive of an expensive perfume: Prelude, Reflective, Eternity, Second Thoughts.

The golfer can play the course for a green fee during the winter of $175 (with a golf car). A round of golf probably will take at least five hours and the golfer will be lucky to lose only a half dozen golf balls and play within ten shots of his or her handicap. When the course was one of the four used in the 1987 Bob Hope Chrysler Classic, the pros of the PGA Tour complained so bitterly about the course's severity and unfairness that in an unprecedented decision Deane R. Beman, commissioner of the PGA Tour, removed the course from the Hope Classic the following year. Nonetheless, the course has achieved a sort of warped fame as the venue for the last six years of the Skins Game, a two-day, made-for-television golf show, whose appeal—like its name—is no more than skin deep.

In the last ten years the Landmark Land Company has been the largest purchaser and developer of land in the Coachella Valley. In 1981 they bought Mis-

1982, when the savings and loan industry was deregulated, Oak Tree Savings Bank was providing loans to Landmark Land and financing to home buyers, which may have seemed imprudent but, nevertheless, at the time was very legal. In the summer of 1989, when the savings and loan debacle reached crisis proportions, a new federal law prohibited any savings and loan institution from owning real estate outright. In 1991 four officers of the Oak Tree Savings Bank were charged with conflict of interest and breach of fiduciary duty.

Twice the Office of Thrift Supervision disapproved of sales of various properties of Landmark Land. On May 1, 1992, in Charleston, South Carolina, Landmark Land filed a disclosure statement with the federal district court that set forth its intention to sell its properties in Oklahoma, Louisiana, and Florida. On June 8 they filed a disclosure statement that set forth their intention to reorganize those properties on Kiawah Island and in California, as a way out of their present situation of operating in bankruptcy. Landmark's timing with the courts could be just right. And as in golf, timing is everything.

Contrast and change: it's all part of life in the Coachella Valley. Yet one thing is predictable—that most unpredictable of things, the weather. Any Saturday morning from December until May the temperature is climbing to a balmy 80 degrees and the humidity is below 20 percent. The air is clear and clean. It's another strawberry sundae of a day.

At the Thunderbird Country Club, former United States President Gerald R. Ford, acting very democratically, will have his name put into a hat and the club's pro, Don Callahan, will randomly select three other golfers. Teams will be made up and the wages will be set. The game is on. This Saturday morning ritual is pervasive across the Coachella Valley.

The men who play are retired or semi-retired. And while every year or so they lose a few more yards off their drives, they relentlessly continue to practice and to play. Many combat an arthritic pivot on their drives and frayed nerves on the putting green. But they participate. They believe in the sign posted on many a pro shop wall which reads, THOSE WHO DO NOT FIND TIME FOR EXERCISE, FIND TIME FOR ILLNESS.

85

sion Hills Country Club and in 1985 acquired La Quinta Country Club. They had Pete Dye design their new Mountain Course, which has become one of the best courses in The Valley and now is ranked 70th on *Golf Digest*'s Greatest Golf Courses listing. With three courses at Mission Hills, three at La Quinta, and four at PGA West, that's 180 holes of desert golf.

Landmark Land Company and its divisions are subsidiaries of Oak Tree Savings Bank of New Orleans, Louisiana. For almost two decades, through Landmark Land, Oak Tree built high-quality, well-managed, and very profitable developments around golf courses. In

# PEBBLE BEACH

**L**ast summer while the residents of Southampton, New York, were enjoying a glorious, rainless summer behind their tall hedges, the residents of Northern California's Pebble Beach—located 125 miles south of San Francisco—were also experiencing a warm, rainless but untypically fogless summer and the continuation of a five-year drought. They were not basking in it, but were bitterly complaining. Finally, when the weather temporarily changed around mid-July, one of the residents summed up most of the prevalent feelings about what is considered proper Pebble Beach weather. He gazed down the famous 18th fairway of Pebble Beach Golf Links and watched as it was quickly covered by a blanket of fog.

"Isn't it beautiful," he said.

He didn't mean the 18th hole, which indeed is beautiful and has been the site of some of golf's most heroic and bizarre moments. "Anyone who loves Pebble Beach also must love the fog."

Fog is to Pebble Beach what the tall hedges are to Southampton. It helps to ensure privacy and exclusion, and in a murky way is even a discriminating factor. Though the family tree of many a Pebble Beach resident is a twisted and tortured affair, there are strong ancestral ties to gloom, beauty, and splendor, accounted for by the area's substantial population of people of English, Irish, and Scottish descent. They and the fog have produced a sportive social climate for formal informality. Here social pretension is met with ridicule. Once, when the Duchess of Manchester was first married to her second husband William H. Crocker, she insisted on being called Elizabeth rather than Liz. The Pebble Beach residents considered this a rather banal affectation. They retaliated by calling her "Betty Crocker."

Besides the fog, rain, wind and the brilliant, sunny days of spring and fall, there's the Del Monte forest, thick with cypress, oak, and pine trees, a hauntingly beautiful place where deer roam free from the threat of the stalking hunter. In fact, the area is a sanctuary of wildlife. Sea gulls, geese, and duck flock the cliffs and litter the fairways. A bark of a bull seal has interrupted the quietest backswing.

Then there's the shore, called "the greatest meeting of land and water in the world" by Robert Louis Stevenson. Thus, to the residents of Pebble Beach, the most important thing about Pebble Beach is Pebble Beach itself, which many inhabitants call the noblest coastline in the world. There are the majestic headlands with wind-seared cliffs dropping 300 feet into Carmel Bay. The craggy zigzagging shoreline is pounded by waves that have been building up hundreds of miles off-shore and come rolling in to spend their fury on the rocky coast. An occasional hidden crescent-shaped beach punctuates the wild coastline. All these famous views are from the "17-Mile Drive," a five-dollar toll road that winds circuitously through the most beautiful part of Pebble Beach. It begins on the edge of the Del Monte forest, then runs along the coastline past some grand houses and a tree called "the Lone Cypress." The tree grows hard on a piece of land that juts into the Pacific; it's a tree battered by strong ocean winds, and the spray from the ocean. It's held together here and there by wire. It grows against odds, and its meaning is rooted deeply: a reverence for all living things.

Pebble Beach today, with its inbred pockets of society and a smattering of the affluent show-business celebrities, owes much to the guiding spirit of Samuel F.B. Morse. He was one of the first men to lure home buyers—actually the coterie of California's Big Four families, the Crockers, Huntingtons, Stanfords, and Hopkinses—by selling real estate around golf courses: Pebble Beach Golf Links and Cypress Point Club. He once told a real estate salesman, "Don't sell any property unless you feel that you're doing the buyer a favor."

That saying would ripple through the Monterey Peninsula until his death in 1969. And his powerful legacy, that the Pebble Beach Golf Links should be open to the public and the area not be overdeveloped, doomed a Japanese developer twenty-three years after Morse's death.

It was a decision that would have made Morse proud. He was the man who envisioned Pebble Beach, and nurtured it environmentally with great care for over fifty years. He was the grand-nephew of the primitive

painter and inventor of the telegraph, Samuel Morse. Keen on physical fitness, Samuel F.B. Morse was a fullback and captain of the 1906 Yale football team, serving under Yale's legendary coach (or "graduate adviser" as the position was termed then), Walter Camp. Under Morse's leadership, Yale held its two arch-rivals Harvard and Princeton scoreless. Into middle age, Morse liked to play polo, raise show dogs, and, to prove his physical prowess, tear a telephone book in half.

He maintained a rather unexecutive disdain for hard work and persistence. He once said, "Men do not get along in the world by hard work and perseverance; they keep you from meeting the right people." Thus, Morse was one of the few men in the world who rode horseback with President Theodore Roosevelt, and though a notoriously poor golfer, played golf with President Dwight Eisenhower.

In 1915 at the age of twenty-eight, Morse headed the Pacific Improvement Company, a subsidiary of the Southern Pacific Company. They owned more than 7000 acres on the Monterey Peninsula that they had purchased from an attorney named David Jacks for $5 per acre. To lure train passengers, the railroad had built the Hotel Del Monte, and since the 1890s had promoted the area as the Newport of the West. Their timing was off by fifty years.

Morse's job was to liquidate the holdings at the best price possible. When Morse saw the Monterey Peninsula, he was like a man falling in love for the first time. He wrote rapturously about it: "The effect of the Monterey Peninsula is to make one want to shout, to run rather than walk." He was both a protective and a possessive suitor of the love object. And the more he saw of the property the more he was convinced of its future as a luxurious playground. With financial backing from San Francisco's Fleishhacker family, he formed a consortium and bought the property for $1.3 million.

To lure wealthy settlers to his domain, Morse knew he couldn't offer just another golf course. It would have to be one that would make the peninsula something of a Pinehurst-of-the-West. He thus selected the most dramatic stretch of real estate, already called Pebble Beach, not for home sites as was originally intended, with eighty-foot lots ready to become a Carmel subdivi-

**ABOVE.** The greatest finishing hole in golf: the 540-yard, par-5 18th at Pebble Beach Golf Links. **LEFT.** Cobina Carolyn "C.C." Beaudette at the Pebble Beach Equestrian Center.

**PHOTO PAGE 86.** The breathtakingly beautiful 10th hole at Pebble Beach Golf Links. On the right is Carmel Bay.

90

ABOVE. Actress Jeanne Eagels playing at Pebble Beach Golf Links in 1926. RIGHT. Douglas Fairbanks and Mary Pickford at Pebble Beach in 1929. BELOW RIGHT. Samuel F.B. Morse, the guiding spirit behind Pebble Beach.

sion, but for a golf course.

Morse hired Jack Neville to design the course. Neville had won the California Amateur in 1912 and 1913. (He would win again in 1919, 1922, and 1929.) The fact that Neville had never designed a tee, a bunker, or a green didn't bother Morse. He felt any man who could play golf as well as Neville could design a decent course. In *The New Yorker*, Herbert Warren Wind wrote, "The truth is neither Morse nor Neville knew what they had. Pebble Beach really is one of golf's happiest accidents."

Neville's course forms an elongated figure eight, a design that architecturally takes the fullest advantage of the coastline. The 4th hole, and then holes six through ten, are the first of the fearsome ocean holes, stretching along headlands. The greens and tees are pitched by the cliff's edge. With the 11th hole, the course loops inland, becomes a bit more mellow, and with the 17th and 18th holes, again returns to the ocean. The bow-shaped, 540-yard, par-5 18th, with an often stormy Carmel Bay splashing against the sea wall from the tee to the green, is as fitting a final statement to the course as the cannon fire is to the finale of the *1812 Overture*.

Neville hired Douglas Grant, another Yale graduate (he would go on to win the 1918 California Amateur) to help him with the design of the greens and the bunkering. The greens they designed were small and flat and the bunkering around them was neither inspiring nor very strategic. Although Neville's routing has remained almost the same, the course then was quite different than it is today. The 9th was a short par 4 and the 10th was a par-5 dogleg right along the cliffs. The 16th green was left of the barrancas, and the 18th was an uninspiring 370-yard par 4.

When Morse accepted the bid for the 1929 U.S. Amateur, he hired M. Chandler Egan to redesign the course. Egan had won the 1904 and 1905 U.S. Amateurs and had designed several courses in the northwest. Egan lengthened the par-4 9th and redesigned the 10th, from a par 5 into a stern 436-yard par 4. He moved the green on the 16th beyond the barranca. And—most of all—he redesigned the 18th and made it the most dramatic finishing hole in golf.

The 1929 Amateur was memorable for three things: in the very first round, Bobby Jones was beaten 1-up by Johnny Goodman. Jones's Boswell, O.B. Keeler, wrote philosophically: "Golf championships are a good deal like omelets. You cannot have an omelet without breaking eggs and you cannot have a golf championship without wrecking hopes."

Instead of going home and feeling sorry for himself, Jones actually stayed around. He went over to play the Cypress Point Course, which would lead to his hiring Alister Mackenzie to design Augusta National Golf Club. He also refereed the third-round match between Harrison R. Johnston and George J. Voight. Egan, though in his mid-forties, proved he could still play as he reached the semifinals. The final was memorable for one shot. In the morning round on the 18th, Johnston went for the green, with his second shot a brassie; he hooked the ball badly and it sailed into Carmel Bay. But the tide was out and he found his ball on the beach. He played a splendid recovery with a spade mashie (six-iron) to the green and saved his par. He won 4 and 3.

Ah, the 18th. It has been the battleground of some of the most bizarre and heroic golf. In the final of the 1929 California Amateur, Neville holed a shot from the bunker left of the green for an eagle and victory. Even more spectacular was the shot in the 1952 Crosby Pro-Am. The pro, Art Bell, and his partner Bill Hoelle, came to the last green with an outside chance of tying. Hoelle put his second shot in the bunker near the sea wall. From there he elected to play a seven-iron shot. He holed it, for an eagle and victory.

Then there was Hale Irwin in the 1984 Crosby. One of the straightest drivers on the PGA Tour, he stood on the tee needing a par to tie Jim Nelford. In uncharacteristic fashion he hit a terrible hook and the ball sailed into Carmel Bay, but it hit a rock and bounced onto the fairway. Reaching the green in three shots he two-putted for a par and won the playoff.

However, such heroics are rare. In the 1959 Crosby, Gene Littler played beautiful golf from the 65th to the 71st hole and picked up eight strokes on Art Wall. He needed one last birdie to tie Wall. Calm and confident on the tee, he hit his driver perilously close to the

91

sea wall. Now, somewhat shaken, he nevertheless went for the green with a three-wood and hit a howling hook sending the ball into Carmel Bay. He ended up with an inglorious seven.

And who can forget the 1976 Crosby Pro-Am? After sixty-three holes, Jack Nicklaus was leading and well on his way to winning his fourth Crosby. What happened is still mystifying. It was worse than a rub of the green. It was as if the gods of golf wanted vengeance. Nicklaus took a bogey and then another bogey. At the par-4 13th, his drive ended up in a huge fairway divot. His approach to the green rolled up under a buried stone. It took him two to get on the green and he two-putted for a double bogey. On the par-3 17th, a capricious wind came up just as he hit his tee shot and his ball was buried in the face of the bunker. It took him two shots to get the ball to the green and two more putts for another double bogey. On the 18th, after a good drive, Nicklaus went for the green in two, and hooked his shot into Carmel Bay. He finished with another double bogey for a nine-hole score of a very un-Nicklauslike 45.

Down to the last slippery putt, Egan's design fulfilled Morse's expectations—and he was a man of grand expectations. He once attempted to move the California state capital from Sacramento to Monterey, because he believed it belonged there, since it had been the capital when the Spanish and Mexicans ruled the territory. During World War II, when the U.S. Navy had taken over the Hotel Del Monte as a flight training center, Morse promoted the idea of moving the United States Naval Academy from Annapolis to Monterey. Neither scheme worked. Nor did his rather ingenious scheme of fertilizing his golf fairways in 1931 by using guano scraped from the rocks frequented by the cormorants and pelicans. It not only proved damaging to the fairways, but once the rocks were cleaned, the seals took possession and the birds never came back. He also attempted to introduce elk to the area. That proved disastrous, particularly when a male and female decided to mate on the 7th green at Cypress Point Club and almost tore it to bits.

Though Morse headed the California delegation for the Democratic nomination of Alf Landon in 1936, his own politics could be called baronial. Indeed, his so-

briquet was "the Duke of Monterey." He told aspiring residents what kind of houses they could or could not build and where not to cut down a cypress tree. During the 1920s and the 1930s, only houses of Mediterranean or Italian style could be built along the coastline, because from out on Carmel Bay he wanted the shore to look like the Mediterranean Riviera.

Movie producers as well as residents have found the place intoxicatingly beautiful. Those in search of an angry sea, eerie fog, or pristine landscape have filmed Pebble Beach. The original *National Velvet* starring Elizabeth Taylor was filmed there. The Riviera scenes in *Intermezzo* were filmed there, and the road scenes of Alfred Hitchcock's *Vertigo* were shot over "17-Mile Drive." And almost all of Clint Eastwood's first directorial attempt, *Play Misty for Me*, was filmed in Pebble Beach and Carmel.

In 1947 the Bing Crosby Pro-Am moved from its original site since 1937, the Ranch Santa Fe Country Club in San Diego, to Pebble Beach. The original three courses there were Cypress Point Club, Monterey Peninsula Country Club, and Pebble Beach Golf Links. In 1967 Spyglass Hill Golf Course replaced Monterey Peninsula and in 1991 Poppy Hills Golf Course replaced Cypress Point Club. If Pebble Beach was good for the tournament, offering the pro and the amateur great golf in a great setting, the tournament was good for Pebble Beach. Traditionally, the tournament is played in January, a month noted for foul weather on the Monterey Peninsula—high winds, rain, and even occasionally snow. Once a slow season, the tournament filled up the Del Monte Lodge and brought in spectators.

While Morse was a man of warmth and easy charm, he was utterly uncompromising when it came to his vision of what Pebble Beach should be. However, this Duke of Monterey consistently exercised a spirit of noblesse oblige when it came to the use of Pebble Beach Golf Links, especially for amateurs. The California Amateur has been held there every year since 1929, the California Women's Amateur six times, and the California Open eleven times. After World War II, while many courses were slowly recovering from neglect during the war years, Pebble Beach was put in top shape almost immediately, and it played host to the 1947 U.S. Ama-

**ABOVE.** The most photographed golf hole at Cypress Point—the 233-yard, par-3 16th. A. Thomas Taylor *(left)* and Bing Crosby happily signify that they've both scored a rare hole-in-one. **LEFT.** Clint Eastwood near his home in Pebble Beach.

94

**ABOVE.** Jack Nicklaus, on his way to winning the 1972 Open at Pebble Beach. **RIGHT.** Tom Kite, 1992 Open Champion.

**OVERLEAF.** The beguiling 120-yard, par-3 7th hole at Pebble Beach.

teur in which Robert H. (Skee) Riegel beat Johnny Dawson 2 and 1. The following year Pebble Beach played host to the Women's Amateur in which Grace S. Lenczk beat Helen Sigel 4 and 3.

The 1961 U.S. Amateur that was played at Pebble Beach was historic. It attracted the largest number of entries, 1995 golfers, of any Amateur. The favorite, Jack Nicklaus, won. He had won that year's NCAA golf championship and the 1959 U.S. Amateur. Playing some of the best golf of his young career, he beat H. Dudley Wysong Jr. in the final 8 and 6. And there in the west, the dawn broke on a new era in golf—the Nicklaus era.

The 1972 and 1982 U.S. Opens played at Pebble Beach were similar in the drama and the champions they produced: Jack Nicklaus in 1972 and Tom Watson in 1982. At the time, each man was thirty-two years of age and had been playing the PGA Tour for ten years. They were both at the peak of their careers. Nicklaus already had won fifteen major championships and Watson five. Both men played with great skill, heart, and courage. And while it often is stated that nobody ever wins the U.S. Open, everybody else loses it, that definitely was not the case with Nicklaus and Watson. They both decisively won the championship, and when they felt the starch of competition, hit a great shot.

"It was the best shot I have ever played at Pebble Beach," Nicklaus says. "In fact, one of the best shots I have ever played." "It was," says Watson, "easier to hole the shot than to get it close." Such is the thump of confidence. Nicklaus, of course, was referring to the one-iron shot he hit during the final round on the par-3 17th hole. Although he had a three-shot lead over Bruce Crampton, anything can happen on the hole. Into a near gale wind Nicklaus took out a one-iron. The ball screamed into the wind and into history. The ball hit one foot from the hole, bounced, hit the flagstick and stopped five inches from the hole. He had his birdie, and although he would bogey the 18th hole he still won by three shots.

When Watson stood on the 17th tee during the final round, he was tied with Nicklaus, who already had completed play at four under par. Watson played a two-iron. The ball hooked a tad too much, hit the left side of the green and bounced into the tall rough fifteen feet from the hole. It seemed that all the hard work of the week was going to be undone by one sloppy shot. But when Watson looked at the lie, he was relieved. Instead of the ball nestling deep in the grass it was sitting up, and he could work a sand wedge under it. After twice adjusting his stance, he swung. The ball popped up, landed on the collar of the green and rolled quickly toward the hole, hit the flagstick, and dropped in the hole. Instead of a four, he had a birdie 2 and a one-stroke lead. He played the par-5 15th with a three-wood off the tee, a seven-iron, and a full nine-iron to the green. He holed his final putt for a birdie four and a two-shot victory.

The 1992 U.S. Open at Pebble Beach was different but in its own way equally as historic as the other two Opens. It wasn't won by a major player at the very peak of his career, but by one of the most consistent golfers over the last twelve years on the PGA Tour. Tom Kite at the age of forty-two played some of the steadiest golf of his career, with only two shots separating his best and worst round. He shot a final-round par of 72 in howling winds for a total of three-under-par 285. It was the 17th victory of his career and his 21st attempt at the Open championship.

In 1994, the U.S. Amateur will be played at Pebble Beach for the first time since 1961. It will be, including the 1977 PGA Championship played there, the 9th championship at Pebble Beach. The Amateur will begin the USGA's year-long celebration of its centennial. An ironic touch in the celebration hasn't been lost on the Pebble Beach residents. A century ago Pebble Beach was often referred to as the Newport of the West. The site of the 1995 Amateur is the Newport Country Club in Newport, Rhode Island.

The history of Pebble Beach after Morse died in 1969 has been as dramatic and unpredictable as any final round in an Open championship. Less than ten years after Morse died the Pebble Beach Corporation was sold to Twentieth Century-Fox for $72 million. Significantly, the sale was approved only when Fox agreed it would operate Pebble Beach "in the same management philosophy, style, and tradition" as Morse. That decision would reverberate through the future decades. In 1981 Marvin Davis, a self-made oilman and one of the richest men in America, purchased Twentieth

95

98

The par-3 16th hole at Cypress Point.

Century-Fox for $722 million and with it came Pebble Beach, then valued at $150 million. Believing his property would be worth even more, he supervised the building of the elegant Inn at Spanish Bay and the links at Spanish Bay. During the heady 1980s real estate was rocketing upward in value, and in 1990 Davis sold Pebble Beach to Japanese businessman Minoru Isutani for $841 million. The sale included Pebble Beach Golf Links, the Lodge at Pebble Beach, the Peter Hay par-3 Pitch and Putt course, Spyglass Hill Golf Course, the Links at Spanish Bay, and the Inn at Spanish Bay.

The sale had the same impact on American golfers as a shanked shot. Isutani's business reputation was at best unsavory. To finance the deal he borrowed $574 million from the Mitsubishi Trust and Banking Corporation. Isutani had plans for the privatization of Pebble Beach. He would sell memberships in the Pebble Beach Golf Links to the Japanese for $750,000 each. The money would finance 900 new homes, a new hotel, and a golf course. Such plans were contrary to the legacy of Samuel F.B. Morse. The news was to environmentalists what blood is to a vampire. In October 1991 the California Coastal Commission voted 10 to 1 rejecting the proposal. Andrew Pollack wrote in *The New York Times,* "The members of the coastal commission, a state agency that regulates coastal development, said that selling the memberships to play the ritzy course at prime times would restrict the public's access to the shoreline, which it is charged with protecting."

Without a cash flow to pay the heavy debt of $841 million, Isutani's company was in trouble. It missed a $3-million tax payment to Monterey County. Finally, the Sumitomo Bank took control and arranged for Isutani to sell the property to the Taiheiyo Club, Inc., which was operated by the highly respectable Masatsugu Takabayashi. The price was $500 million. Isutani and his backers lost $341 million. Takabayashi vowed to restore Pebble Beach to the vision of Samuel Morse. He formed a parent company to run the day-by-day operations of the property called the Lone Cypress Company which, with himself, two other Japanese and two Americans formed a cross-cultural team. In the end, one man's vision had endured over time and money.

When the Isutani incident finally ended, the members of the Cypress Point Club just up the road, one of the most exclusive clubs in the world, let out a collective sigh of relief. To them, Pebble Beach is already too crowded, and the demands to play their course by guests is so staggering that more than a decade ago the club inaugurated a policy that each member can have only three guests during the year. To them, there was always the specter that they could be next.

For sheer physical beauty, there are few courses in the world more beautiful than Cypress Point. The course is situated at the tip of the Monterey Peninsula and stretches along the palisades above the Pacific Ocean. The inland holes, one through fourteen, are played among sand dunes and in the quiet beauty of the forest, with fairways lined with cypress and pine trees. The course's most spectacular stretch is holes 15 through 17, played among the headlands above the Pacific.

Just as the Old Course at St. Andrews seems to inspire the Scots to write poetry, Cypress has inspired some of the most lyrical and inspirational descriptive writing. When O.B. Keller, the golf writer for the *Atlanta Journal,* first saw Cypress he wrote, "Cypress Point is a dream—spectacular, perfectly designed, and set about the white sand dunes and a cobalt sea, and studded with the Monterey Cypress, so bewilderingly picturesque that it seems to have been the crystallization of a dream of an artist who had been drinking gin and sobering up on absinthe."

The great British golf writer Pat Ward-Thomas wrote, "No golf architect was more richly endowed with natural features of his work than Alister Mackenzie at Cypress Point—majestic woodlands, a hint of links and heathland here and there and the savage nobility of the coast made for unforgettable holes." More recently American golf writer Cal Brown wrote, "There cannot be another place on earth quite like it. It is as though every thundering motion, every subtle line, had been withheld from the rest of creation and then dumped in this one place to test our understanding of the superlative." Then there was member Frank "Sandy" Tatum, former president of the United States Golf Association and a lawyer, who once wrote in unlawyerlike brevity, "Cypress Point is the Sistine Chapel of Golf."

99

The club was founded in 1928 in what proved to be a mutual coup for those forming the club and Del Monte Properties, who was selling the land. The club brought 167 acres from Del Monte for $116,000 for the exclusive purpose of building a golf course. The club borrowed the money—with interest—from Del Monte, and also borrowed $67,000 to build the clubhouse.

Two people were instrumental in the formation of Cypress Point Club: Roger Lapham and Francis Mc-Comas. Lapham was from a socially prominent San Francisco family and was an outstanding amateur golfer. He convinced the USGA to bring its amateur championship in 1929 to Pebble Beach which, considering that the USGA had never gone farther west than St. Louis for any of its championships, was a quantum jump for them.

At the time Marion Hollins was working for the Del Monte properties. She was a woman of many talents. Born on Long Island's North Shore, she grew up in a golfing atmosphere near such courses as Meadow Brook (site of the first Women's Amateur), Piping Rock Club, and Nassau Country Club. In 1921 Hollins won the Women's Amateur. She also was a feminist, an accomplished horsewoman, a fine tennis player, and the first woman to enter the Vanderbilt Cup, a car race on Long Island. In 1923 she founded the Women's National Golf Club (now the Glen Wood Country Club) in Roslyn, New York. She would later create the Pasatiempo Country Club, the site of the 1987 Women's Amateur. In the mid-1920s she and her family were in Pebble Beach, and Morse hired her as the company's athletic director, and also as a real estate salesperson.

It was Lapham and Hollins who decided to hire Dr. Alister Mackenzie to design the course at Cypress Point. It wasn't a haphazard decision. Although up to that time most of Mackenzie's work had been in Great Britain, he had designed an estate golf course for Charlie Chaplin, and more importantly had designed the Dunes Course at Monterey Peninsula Country Club. His work also was being praised by Robert Hunter, who had written a classic book on golf course architects titled *The Links*. It was Hunter who had persuaded Mackenzie to come to California, and often assisted him, though there was no formal partnership.

For all Cypress's majestic beauty it does have several architectural anomalies. It has two back-to-back par 5s, the 490-yard 5th and the 521-yard 6th; it also has two back-to-back par 3s, the 139-yard 15th and 233-yard 16th. Also, the finishing hole is weak, a 339-yard, uphill, dog-leg right par 4. And the course only stretches 6464 yards and plays to a par 72.

Like Seminole Golf Club just north of Palm Beach, Cypress Point dislikes publicity. However, Cypress has gone further than Seminole in supporting golf and particularly amateur golf. From 1947 until 1990, one round of the Crosby Pro-Am—later replaced in 1986 by the AT&T Pebble Beach National Pro-Am—was played over Cypress. In 1981 the Walker Cup Matches were played there with the U.S. team beating Great Britain and Ireland 15 to 9. And until 1990, two qualifying rounds of the California State Amateur were played there.

If the club's golfing policies seem circumscribed, its social tone is more so. It was stabilized early on by a local painter and founding member, Francis McComas. His concept called for a club that should be small—it only has 234 members—and elegant, with perfect food and service, where all the members would be great friends; a sanctuary for the group that first came to Pebble Beach and golfed there before everyone else golfed. The lovely colonial-styled clubhouse is smallish, of white clapboard with green shutters and four great rooms facing the 16th hole.

Once member Bob Hope described the club's membership policy. "Cypress Point is so exclusive that it had a membership drive and drove out forty members." Fewer than sixty members reside in or near the Monterey Peninsula. And while carrying one's own bag usually is discouraged at most clubs as having a plebeian touch, at Cypress Point it actually is encouraged, because walking rather than taking a golf car is urged. The members also observe one of the club's oldest traditions of using only small canvas bags, "Sunday Bags," as they were once called. This isn't meant as reverse snobbism, but as a courtesy to the caddies (and also one's self) whom the members regard as the best on the Monterey Peninsula. And while most clubs have a caddies' day, usually Monday, Cypress Point doesn't. The

**ABOVE.** Roger D. Lapham *(left)* and Charles de Bretteville at the 139-yard, par-3 15th hole at Cypress Point. **RIGHT.** Marion Hollins, winner of the 1921 Women's Amateur.

club's caddies have the distinct privilege, which most of the golfing world would love to enjoy, of being able to play the course almost any afternoon when the course isn't crowded.

If it seems that the caddies are treated better than guests, they often are. Guests aren't allowed in the clubhouse unless they're accompanied by a member. Even then they must be properly attired. This has caused myriad problems. During the 1958 Crosby Pro-Am the junior senator from Massachusetts, Jack Kennedy, watching the day's play, started to enter the clubhouse but was turned away because he was barefoot and wearing Bermuda shorts. Men must wear coat and tie when lunching. Women are requested to be properly attired in the dining room; jeans are never allowed. Until five years ago a stern bylaw was posted in the golf pro shop that defined for the members which wives were not considered members. The bylaw read: "Wives do not include those to whom an interlocutory decree of divorce is outstanding."

Located halfway between Cypress Point Club and Pebble Beach Golf Links is Spyglass Hill golf course. It was opened in 1966 and designed by Robert Trent Jones. Serving his apprenticeship for his father was Robert Trent Jones Jr. The course is very different from its neighbors. It neither has the heroic shot value of the ocean holes at Pebble Beach nor the dramatic beauty of the ocean holes at Cypress Point.

What it does have is a rare hybrid, a mix of two of America's great courses. The first five holes are very reminiscent of Pine Valley. After a thunderous drive off the first tee of the 600-yard par 5, the fairway runs downhill and from then on, through the 5th, the holes play among the sand dunes and ice plants. It's target golf, and when the wind is up, which is usual, it can play havoc with the best shots. At the 6th hole the course moves upward and plays along high ground. With the tall, stately pines lining the broad fairways, there's something of the look of Augusta National. Enhancing the look are four very strategically placed ponds reflecting the tall pines.

The course is semiprivate, and since 1966 was the headquarters of the Northern California Golf Association and the site used for many of their tour-

naments. That changed in 1986 when Poppy Hills opened as the new headquarters and administrative offices and site for the association's tournaments. The course was nine years in the making, since 168 acres high up in the Del Monte forest became available and the NCGA bought it for $1.5 million. It took five years for all the permits to be resolved. Finally in 1982 the Environmental Impact Report was approved with forty-eight conditions attached. Next, the California Coastal Commission gave the project its blessing and added another nineteen conditions.

Robert Trent Jones Jr. designed the course as a fun course that's not too demanding. The course stretches from 5554 yards to 6850 from the championship tees. There are only seventy-seven bunkers and the fairways are amply wide. Tall pine trees frame the fairways and mounds from the contours that lead the eye to the green. Each green is large and undulating and planted with bent Pencross. They can be shaved down to become lightning fast. There are no blind shots to the greens as each is tilted toward the fairway, giving the golfer a very inviting target. The course was named after the California state flower, the poppy. Ironically, when the course was opened not one poppy existed on the course, but the golfers were given packets of seeds and soon the state flower began to bloom and blossom along with the young course.

The newest and final golf course built in Pebble Beach, adjacent to the Monterey Peninsula Country Club, is the Links at Spanish Bay. It signifies a giant step forward into the past. If Augusta National symbolizes the glories of modern American golf course architecture, in which the greens are receptive to high shots and where the game is played in a theatre of stunning beauty with blossoming azaleas and dogwoods, beautiful green fairways, and blue ponds, then the Links at Spanish Bay is its antithesis.

It's more of the past than the present, and more British than American—as if the architects had heard Alistair Cooke reading aloud from Bernard Darwin's *The Golf Courses of the British Isles*. There's the linksland, the tight turf of fescue grass, which allows the golfer to effectively play those exquisite pitch-and-run shots and even those long 100 yard bump-and-run shots. There are

**ABOVE.** An eerie Pebble Beach fog covers the 600-yard, par-5 1st hole at Spyglass Hill Golf Course. **LEFT.** Tom Watson, Robert Trent Jones Jr., and Frank "Sandy" Tatum, the architects of Spanish Bay.

104

sand dunes, mossy hummocks, and moguls, off of which the ball can take a variety of unusual bounces. And there's the wind whipping in off Spanish Bay. Seemingly the only things missing are the Union Jack fluttering in the wind, caddies wearing tweed caps and smoking cigarettes, and a club secretary roaming the grounds who was a former wing commander in the Royal Air Force and whose gruff manner is only humanized by his love of port.

---

**ABOVE.** The 17th at Spanish Bay.

The golf course is situated on the northernmost "point of interest" of the 17-Mile Drive. From the 1930s until 1973 it had been used to mine sand for glassmaking. The forty years of commerce had left the land scraped raw, a bleak and blighted eyesore. Still, only by the narrowest of votes of 5 to 4 did the California Coastal Commission approve the land for a golf course. It was then that a special architectural team went to work. The team proved as unique as the course: golf course architect Robert Trent Jones Jr., U.S. Open and two-time Masters champ; five-time British Open champion Tom Watson; and Frank Tatum, the 1941 NCAA golf champion, Rhodes scholar, San Francisco lawyer, and former president of the USGA. They wanted a course like the linksland courses of Great Britain, essentially treeless and windswept where the ball is hit under the wind, and rolls on the hard turf.

All this was achieved. Huge sand hills were created by bringing down 550,000 cubic yards of sand from a quarry by conveyer belt from two miles away in the Del Monte forest. The dunes border the fairways, and here and there a green is neatly tucked into a dune. The course spreads over 195 acres with fourteen of the holes actually playing in the linksland. Holes 10 through 13 are played inland. Some of the golf holes have a familiar look to them; the 130-yard, par-3 13th, which runs toward the ocean is very reminiscent of the 126-yard 8th at Royal Troon Golf Club, known as the "Postage Stamp," and the 210-yard, par-3 16th is similar to the 17th at Pebble Beach. The course plays from 5287 yards to 6820 yards and the uneven nines par of 35–37.

Whether you're playing the Links at Spanish Bay or Pebble Beach Golf Links, or privileged enough to play Cypress Point Club, on those brilliant spring and fall mornings when the sun has burned through the fog and you can hear the bark of a bull seal and feel the wind off the Pacific, and the fairways glisten green, it all evokes one of the best lines of P.G. Wodehouse, from *Heart of a Goof:* "It was a morning when all nature shouted, 'Fore!'"

# ONE HUNDRED
# YEARS OF THE
# WORLD OF GOLF

For more than a century, *Town & Country* has covered golf in almost every corner of the earth, wherever the lore and the lure of the game prevailed. The magazine's pages have been brightened with the game's beautiful visual appeal in drawings, paintings, and photographs, in black and white and later in color. The game's great champions, both male and female, and great courses, both famous and lesser-known, have been featured in an enormous variety of lifestyle articles. The following pages represent *Town & Country's* eclectic view of this royal and ancient game.

**107**

**LEFT.** A par 3 at the Shinyo Golf Club, Japan. **ABOVE.** A barranca fronts the green of the 182-yard, par-3 14th hole at the Stanford golf course.

**LEFT.** The inviting but treacherous green of the 190-yard, par-3 3rd hole at The Mid-Ocean Club, Bermuda. **BELOW LEFT.** The elevated green of the 362-yard, par-4 16th hole at the Tryall Golf and Beach Club in Montego Bay, Jamaica. **BELOW.** The downhill (and often downwind) 540-yard, par-5 18th on the Plantation Course, the newest and third course at Kapalua on Maui.

**BELOW.** The azalea-rimmed 13th hole at Augusta, site of the 1989 Masters. **BELOW LEFT.** The perfect follow-through. Bobby Jones practicing in 1934 for the first Masters. **BELOW RIGHT.** Three greats at Augusta National Golf Club *(left to right):* polo player Devereux Milburn, Bobby Jones, and sportswriter Grantland Rice.
**RIGHT.** The 485-yard, par-4 downhill 10th at Augusta. Its name is Camellia.

114

ABOVE. Westchester County's famous Turnesa brothers. Here are six of the seven brothers *(left to right):* Douglas, Philip, James, Frank, Joseph, and Michael. James won the 1952 PGA Championship. RIGHT. A young Dick Chapman shakes hands with U.S. and British Amateur champion Jess Sweetser.

PRECEDING PAGES. The 367-yard, par-4 3rd hole at Ocean Course, site of the 1991 Ryder Cup matches, at Kiawah Island Resort, South Carolina.

**ABOVE.** Winged Foot Golf Club member Dick Chapman won the U.S. Amateur at the club in 1940. **LEFT.** One of the great par 3's in America, the 190-yard 10th of the West Course at Winged Foot Golf Club.

118

**LEFT.** The green of the 408-yard, par-4 4th at Quaker Ridge Golf Club in Westchester County. In the background is the 169-yard, par-3 5th hole. **BELOW LEFT.** At the Sleepy Hollow Country Club above the Hudson River are two former presidents of the USGA: James Hand *(front)* and William J. Williams Jr. **BELOW.** The teacher and his pupils. Winged Foot Golf Club's legendary professional, Claude Harmon *(center, second row),* with *(front row)* Dave Marr, H. Dee, John Burke; *(center row)* Al Mengert and Otto Greiner; *(top row)* Shelly Mayfield, Jay Riviere, and Dick Mayer.

**ABOVE.** Members of St. Andrew's celebrating the club's 50th birthday in 1939. *(Left to right):* Alexander B. Halliday, C. Gary Harris, Percival Wilds, Peter Fletcher, and Archibald Reid. **RIGHT.** John Reid *(right),* founder of New York's St. Andrew's Gold Club, celebrating the club's 25th anniversary with his son, Archibald. **FAR RIGHT.** The Apawamis Club, Rye, New York, celebrating its 50th anniversary in 1940. *(Left to right):* former Apawamis caddie Gene Sarazen; Ben Hogan; Ellis Knowles, the club's excellent amateur golfer; and Leonard Martin.

Wakagi Golf Course, Japan.

124

**ABOVE.** Don't slice. . . . The demanding par-4, 436-yard 7th hole at
Florida's Deering Bay Yacht & Country Club. **ABOVE LEFT.** The Key
Biscayne Golf Club, site of an annual tournament on the Senior
PGA Tour.
**LEFT.** La Garce Country Club, founded in 1927 and still one of the
very best courses in Miami Beach, Florida.

126

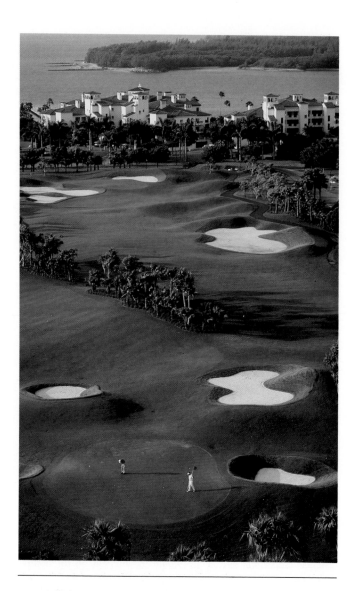

**ABOVE.** The unique nine-hole golf course at Fisher Island, Florida, formerly the William K. Vanderbilt estate.
**RIGHT.** Swaying palms line the fairways of the Acapulco Princess Golf Course in Acapulco, Mexico.

**OVERLEAF.** A grand panoramic view from the fairway of the 545-yard, par-5 3rd hole of the Pevero Golf Club, Sardinia, Italy.

**ABOVE.** The beautiful and challenging 384-yard, par-4 18th hole of the Plainfield Country Club, Plainfield, New Jersey. **LEFT.** It's all carry over a beautiful blue pond to the green of the 194-yard, par-3 4th of the Lower Course at Baltusrol Golf Club, Springfield, New Jersey. It will be the site of the 1993 U.S. Open. **FAR LEFT.** The 133-yard, par-3 12th at the Somerset Hills Country Club, Far Hills, New Jersey. The club hosted the 1990 Curtis Cup Matches.

132

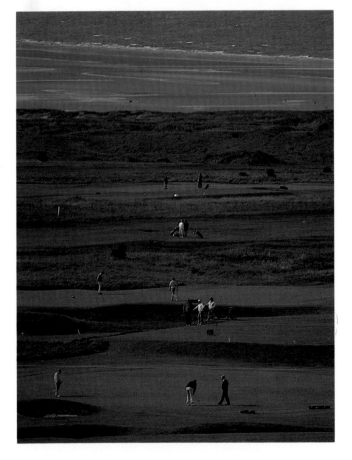

**ABOVE.** Panoramic view of the Old Course with the village of St. Andrews in the background. **ABOVE LEFT.** Still making clubs by hand at the Auchterlonies golf shop. **LEFT.** A unique view of the 4th green and 5th tee of the Old Course, with the New Course and the North Sea. **FAR LEFT.** In the summer gloaming, the clubhouse of the Royal and Ancient Golf Club.

**133**

134

**ABOVE**. The Duke of Windsor *(left)* with Lord Castlerosse *(right)* during the 1933 Autumn Meeting of the Royal and Ancient Golf Club, St. Andrews, Scotland. **RIGHT**. Michael F. Bonnallack, O.B.E., Secretary of the Royal and Ancient Golf Club and five-time British Amateur champion. **FAR RIGHT**. Bing Crosby *(left)* playing in the 1950 British Amateur at St. Andrews. His opponent is J.K. Wilson.

**LEFT.** About to tee off *(left to right):* George S. Moore, Jaime Ortiz-Patino, and Lord Keith of Castleacre, former chairman of Rolls-Royce, at the Valderrama Golf Club on the Costa del Sol, Spain. **FAR LEFT.** The Lido Golf Course, Venice, Italy.

**137**

**ABOVE.** Hitting to the green of the 361-yard, par-4 5th hole at the Club de Golf, Sotorgrande, Spain.
**RIGHT.** With the Sierra Blanca in the background, golf has a grand setting on Spain's Costa del Sol.

138

**ABOVE.** The glorious setting of the 405-yard, par-4 17th green of the Wild Dunes Links Course, Isle of Palms, South Carolina.
**LEFT.** You'd better gauge your tee shot perfectly, or the ball will land in the delicate wetlands or the bunker on the 196-yard, par-3 15th hole of the Calibogue Course at the Haig Point Club, Daufuski Island, South Carolina. **FAR LEFT.** A precise approach shot to the green must avoid the grass hollow *(right)* on the 363-yard, par-4 2nd hole at the Deer Creek Golf Club, The Landing at Skidway Island, Savannah, Georgia.

**ABOVE LEFT.** Bobby Jones in 1930 with his four Grand Slam trophies. He won the U.S. and British Opens as well as the U.S. and British Amateurs. **ABOVE.** Glenna Collett Vare wins her unprecedented sixth Women's Amateur Championship in 1935 at the Interlochen Country Club. Presenting the trophy is USGA president Prescott Bush. **RIGHT.** Golf's big four: Gary Player, Jack Nicklaus, Arnold Palmer, and Tom Watson at the first Skins Game, Desert Highlands, Scottsdale, Arizona.

**OVERLEAF.** Water and more water guards the green of the 477-yard, par-4 12th hole at the Country Club of the Rockies, Edwards, Colorado.

146

**ABOVE.** Five-time British Open Champion Tom Watson proudly displays the trophy to his wife, Linda, in 1980 after winning his third championship at Muirfield. **LEFT.** The great bunkering surrounding the green of the 447-yard, par-4 18th at Muirfield. In the background is the clubhouse of the Honourable Company of Edinburgh Golfers, founded in 1744.

148

**ABOVE.** The 386-yard, par-4 18th green at Royal Lytham and St. Annes, Lancashire, England. **ABOVE LEFT.** A lone golfer hits to the green of the 490-yard, par-5 5th green of the Ailsa Course at the Turnberry Hotel, in Strathclyde, Scotland. In the background is the Ailsa Craig rock. **LEFT.** The famous Postage Stamp Hole, the 126-yard, par-3 8th at Troon Golf Club, Strathclyde, Scotland.

**ABOVE.** Don't hook your tee shot here—the beautiful and precise 154-yard, par-3 13th at the Atlanta Country Club, site of an annual tournament on the PGA Tour. **LEFT.** If you can dance you can play golf. . . . No one proved that adage better than the great Fred Astaire, who played golf in the 70s. Here he is near the 1st tee at the Palmetto Golf Club. **FAR LEFT.** The heart of Amen Corner, the 155-yard, par-3 12th at the Augusta National Golf Club.

152

**ABOVE.** Approaching the green on the 502-yard, par-5 12th North Course at Kaanapali, Maui. **RIGHT.** Countess Court H. Reventlow at Rhode Island's Newport Country Club in 1951.

**153**

**ABOVE.** A solitary golfer drives to the green of the 361-yard, par-4 13th at Cypress Point Club in 1928. **LEFT.** Sartorially attired Scottish caddies Jeffrey Austin *(left)* and friend at the Wade Hampton Golf Club in Cashiers, North Carolina.

**OVERLEAF.** One of the great seaside golf holes in the world, the 385-yard, par-4 8th of the Cajuiles at Casa de Campo, La Romana, Dominican Republic.

154

**ABOVE.** The vagaries of tee time in England, as depicted by Ronald Searle. **RIGHT AND FAR RIGHT.** Texas golfers, by Ronald Searle.

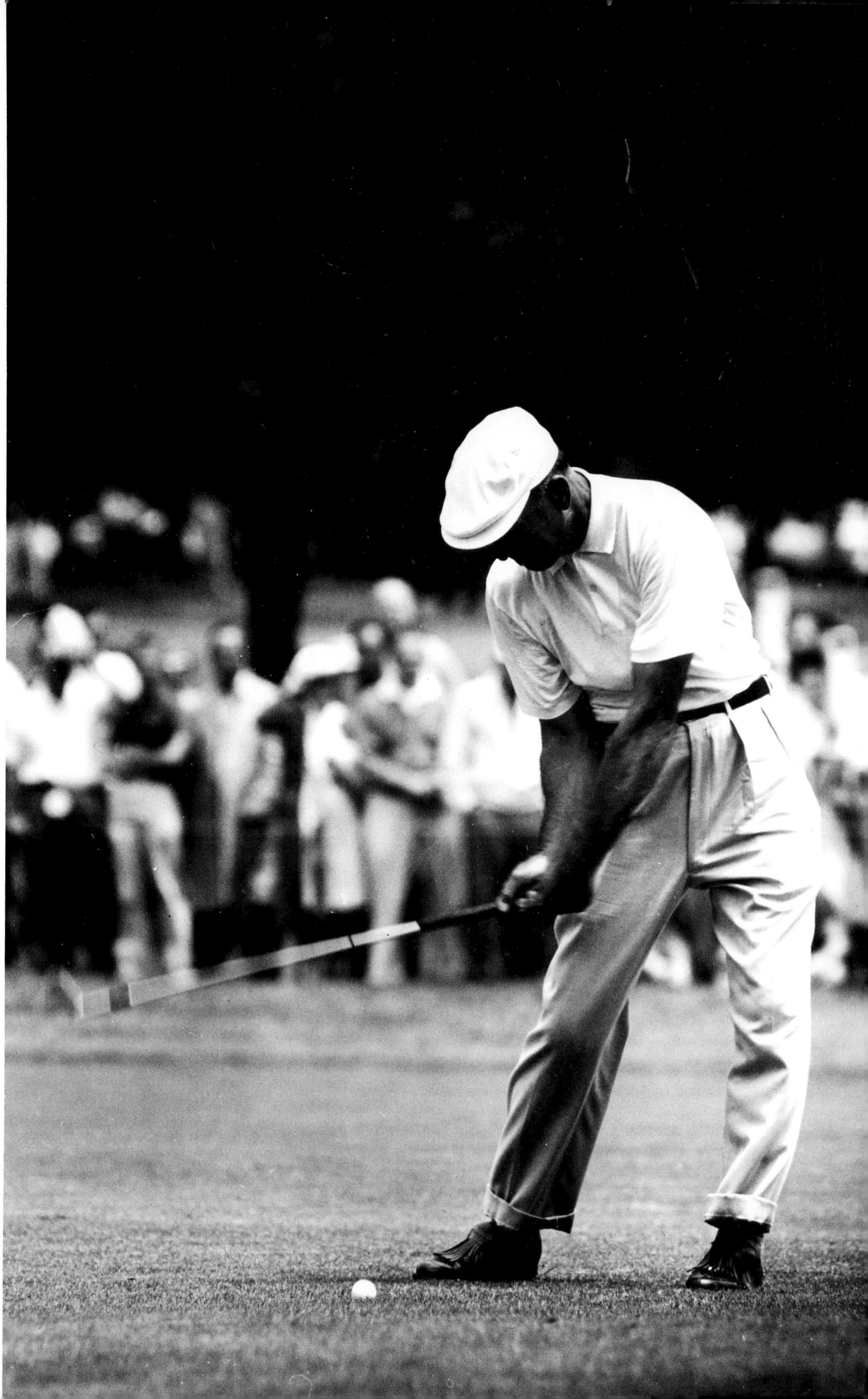

158

**LEFT.** Ben Crenshaw, two-time winner of the PGA Tour event at the Colonial Country Club, with Martha Leonard, daughter of Marvin Leonard, who founded the club in 1935. They are shown in the club's Ben Hogan Trophy Room. **FAR LEFT.** Look and envy: Ben Hogan approaches impact. Note the right heel still on the ground and the bowed left wrist.

159

**OVERLEAF.** The inviting green of the 140-yard, par-3 12th hole at the Golden Horseshoe Golf Course, Williamsburg, Virginia.

162

**ABOVE.** The Northgate Golf Course, Reno, Nevada. **LEFT.** The well-guarded 6th green at Harbour Ridge, Stewart, Florida. **FAR LEFT.** Deer roam the fairways of the Banff Springs Golf Course in the Canadian Rockies.

**ABOVE.** Looking toward the green of the 380-yard, par-4 15th hole at the Paraparumu Beach Golf Club, Wellington, New Zealand. **ABOVE LEFT.** One of five bunkers guarding the green of the 176-yard, par-3 5th hole at Royal Melbourne, Victoria, Australia. **LEFT.** Fences around the greens keep the sheep off the Coromandel Golf Course in New Zealand.

**LEFT.** Looking toward the green of the famed 215-yard, par-3 3rd hole at Mauna Kea Golf Course, Kamuela, Hawaii. **ABOVE.** This is no place to hit a stray approach shot. Nestled among the huge boulders is the green of the 529-yard, par-5 5th hole of the South Course at the Boulders Resort, Carefree, Arizona. **ABOVE RIGHT.** The picturesque and challenging 165-yard, par-3 13th hole at Troon Golf Club, Scottsdale, Arizona.

168

**LEFT.** The 401-yard, par-4 16th at Garden City Golf Club, Garden City, Long Island. The orginal course was designed in 1899 by Devereux Emmet. **BELOW LEFT.** Golf course architect and socialite Devereux Emmet, painted by Rosina Emmet Sherwood in 1929. **BELOW.** On Long Island's fabled North Shore, the tough 450-yard, par-4 14th at the Piping Rock Club.

**ABOVE.** The 228-yard, par-3 15th hole at the spectacular Ballybunion Golf Club, founded in 1896. **LEFT.** Pitching to the green on the 405-yard, par-4 17th hole at the Killarney Golf Club, County Kerry, Ireland. In the background is Lough Leane.

**OVERLEAF.** Royal County Down Golf Club, Newcastle, Northern Ireland. Painting by Frank Magro.

**ABOVE.** Few inland par 3's in the world evoke such salty conversation as the demanding 145-yard 10th at Pine Valley Golf Club. **ABOVE LEFT.** In addition to five bunkers, there's a stream that will catch an errant shot on the 195-yard, par-3 9th at Merion's East Course. **LEFT.** A pushed tee shot will catch this bunker on the 224-yard, par-3 17th at Merion.

**ABOVE.** Five bunkers guard the approach to the green of the 398-yard, par-4 7th hole at the Renegade Course, Desert Mountain Resort, Scottsdale, Arizona. **LEFT.** With the Sierra Nevada Mountains in the background and Lake Tahoe to the right, the 169-yard, par-3 17th is one of the most beautiful holes on Edgewood Golf Course.

178

**ABOVE.** The well-bunkered green of the 162-yard, par-3 10th hole at the Brook Hollow Golf Club, Dallas, Texas. Painting by Arthur Weaver. **ABOVE LEFT.** A Worplesdon club member and his companion watch the finals. **LEFT.** Jill Thornhill, former British Ladies Amateur champion, and two-time member of the Great Britain and Ireland Curtis Cup team. Here she pitches to the 12th green during the semifinals of the 1989 Worplesdon Mixed Foursomes, a competition that dates back to 1921.

180

**ABOVE.** Katharine Hepburn is dazzled by Bobby Jones at a benefit match in 1941. Looking on: Gene Sarazen, Walter Hagen, and Tommy Armour. **ABOVE RIGHT.** At Morocco's Royal Rabat Golf Club, a fashionable woman golfer admires her partner's form. **RIGHT.** Mrs. Richard Fenton holes the winning putt in the snow in St. Moritz, Switzerland.

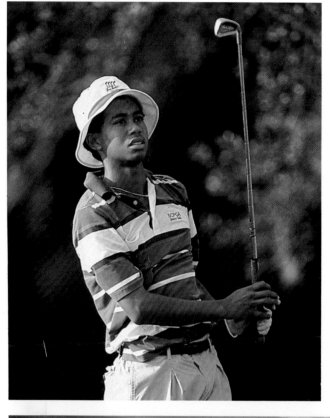

**FAR LEFT.** The demanding 470-yard, par-4 18th at the Castle Pines Golf Club outside Denver, Colorado. Each August, the course is the site of The International, a regular event on the PGA Tour.
**LEFT.** Eldrick "Tiger" Woods winning the 1991 Junior Championship at the Bay Hill Club, Orlando, Florida. **BELOW.** The 460-yard, par-4 18th hole at Bay Hill. Besides hosting the U.S. Amateur and Junior Championship, the club is the site of an annual tournament on the PGA tour.

183

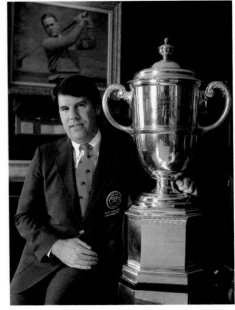

**ABOVE**. Playing to the green of the 8th hole, a 320-yard, par 4 at the Rockaway Hunting Club on Long Island's South Shore. The course was redesigned by Devereux Emmet after World War I. Painting by Frank Magro. **LEFT.** The incomparable and durable Anne Sander. She won the Women's Amateur three times, the Women's Senior Amateur three times, the British Ladies Amateur once, and is the only golfer to play in Curtis Cup Matches for more than five decades. She is shown here at her club, the Broadmoor Golf Club in Seattle, Washington. **BELOW LEFT.** Jay Sigel, one of America's great post-World War II amateurs. He won two U.S. Amateurs, three Mid-Amateurs, a British Amateur, and played on eight U.S. Walker Cup teams. He is shown here with the Walker Cup in the Robert Tyre Jones Jr. Room at Golf House, Far Hills, New Jersey.

186

**ABOVE.** John D. Rockefeller with his 14-year-old grandson, David Rockefeller, in 1930 at Ormond Beach, Florida. **RIGHT.** Payne Stewart, winner of the 1989 PGA Championship and 1991 U.S. Open, with his son Aaron at their home in Orlando, Florida.

**RIGHT.** The tough 440-yard, par-4 3rd hole at The Country Club. In the backgound is the club's skating pond. **BELOW.** Francis Ouimet on his way to winning the 1913 U.S. Open at The Country Club, Boston, Massachusetts. He beat British golfer Harry Vardon and Edward Ray in a playoff.

RIGHT. The Ocean Links, a private nine-hole course in Newport, Rhode Island, owned by T. Suffern Tailer. This 1926 painting is by Paul Moschowitz. BELOW. In 1906 both the automobile and golf were young in America.

**190**

# THE SAGA OF
# COUNTRY CLUB LIFE
# IN AMERICA

Back in the 1920s when the country club was experiencing a great flowering and installing itself as a unique American social institution, an incident occurred at The Country Club in the Boston suburb of Brookline. It confirmed that the country club, with its tribal mores and tidal repetition of form and tradition, had arrived socially. To use one of Boston society's more charming phrases, the country club was now a place where the "well-connected" Bostonian should be.

The incident took place on a balmy Saturday morning in May. A man wearing white flannel knickerbockers, argyle socks, and a white shirt and necktie was about to hit a golf shot off the first tee but was standing a dozen paces in front of the markers, the proper place from which to drive. A long-time member of the club noticed this infraction, approached the golfer, and reproachfully stated that such a breach of the rules of golf simply could not be tolerated at The Country Club. He then went into a brief history of the club—that it was founded in 1882, was the oldest country club still in existence in the United States and that it was, along with Shinnecock Hills Golf Club, St. Andrew's Golf Club, Chicago Golf Club, and Newport Golf Club, among the original charter member clubs of the United States Golf Association in 1894. Continuing in a voice that sounded as if "a flock of sheep had run through his vocabulary," he stated that it was here at The Country Club in 1913 that a former club caddie, Francis Ouimet, beat the great British golfers Harry Vardon and Ted Ray in a playoff to win the U.S. Open, and thus put golf on the front page of newspapers. While motioning for the golfer to return to the tee markers, the man sternly said, "If you can't abide by the rules of golf, the board of governors will accept your resignation immediately."

The bewildered golfer stared angrily at the man for a moment and then said, "Look, you son of a bitch, I've been a member of this club for six months. You're the first member who has spoken to me. And furthermore, I'm about to play my second shot."

The incident is legendary, and while it could

**194**

have occurred at 2500 other country clubs in the United States, it did not. The incident says much about how Boston society guards its boundaries and the social intricacies of the proper Bostonian's club life.

When Harvey Bundy, a Boston Brahmin and the father of McGeorge Bundy (the youngest dean of the arts and sciences faculty at Harvard, and special assistant for national security from 1961 to 1966), was first admitted to Boston's famed Somerset Club—a city club founded in 1851—he lunched alone for nearly a month. Finally, one afternoon as he was having dessert, a member sat at his table. For fifteen minutes they carried on a most pleasant conversation. When the member departed, Mr. Bundy was a happy man, feeling at last he had been fully accepted. But his happiness was short-lived. Five minutes later the man returned and said, "I must apologize, Mr. Bundy, but I thought you were someone else."

It was in this austere and proper environment of Boston, in a society purported to be the most exclusive of any city in America and where it was often said, "Leisure is looked upon as the larceny of time that belongs to other people," that the country club was spawned and nurtured. Under such conditions it seemed unlikely that this social institution of such reticular structure would be nourished by Bostonians and become nationally accepted.

But in the 1880s Boston had something of which it was very proud: its society. Everybody was either in it or out of it; those who were in it proudly guarded their boundaries. They played among themselves—not with others; they competed among themselves—not with others; and above all, they married only among themselves and their children carried on the tradition. Without such a society, the founding of the country club would have been an invalid social exercise.

Unlike the English hunting, shooting, and golfing clubs with their often spartan ambience, the country club originated as a patrician playground loosely modeled on great English country mansions and their leisurely weekends. A keen social critic at the turn of the century observed that the country club, with its sprawling clubhouse and its servants, and its vast acreage of manicured lawns, was the result of the fact that the

---

**PHOTO PAGE 192.** The main ballroom at the Rivercrest Country Club, Fort Worth, Texas.

United States, unlike Great Britain, had no system of primogeniture that would favor the maintenance of great country estates.

It was a piercingly accurate observation. Some measure of the rise of the country is due to the decline of the great country estates once thought to be inviolable. On Long Island's North Shore, monumental maintenance expenses, taxes, and death have led to the replacement of little estate signs bearing such names as Whitney, Vanderbilt, and Burden with larger ones. Respectively, they bear these names: Old Westbury Golf & Country Club, Pine Hollow Country Club, and Woodcrest Club. In 1927 in Charlottesville, Virginia, the Farmington Estate was purchased by Farmington, Inc., for the purpose of forming a country club. Its estate house, one of the most beautiful and now the clubhouse, was designed in 1803 by Thomas Jefferson. In 1955, in Hillsborough, California, the Burlingame Country Club acquired the William H. Crocker New Place Estate. The main house, which became the clubhouse, was designed by Lewis F. Hobart, the designer of Grace Cathedral in San Francisco. The sprawling three-story clubhouse (designed by Stanford White) at the Sleepy Hollow Country Club in Scarborough-On-Hudson, New York, was the summer mansion of Colonel Eliot Shepard, who was married to Margaret Louisa Vanderbilt, one of the four daughters of William Henry Vanderbilt.

While country clubs may appear rigid in time and tradition, they have proved themselves to be a remarkably flexible social institution. They have survived a century of tumultuous change in America. They survived the depression of 1893, World War I, the Great Depression of the 1930s, World War II, the anti-establishment decade of the 1960s, and the endless conflicts between civil rights groups and the claimants of social right of private association. Clubs have survived (if at a different location) federal and state highway programs, as well as their chief nemesis, the local tax assessor. Clubs have survived their own members and committees. They have even survived Groucho Marx, who once said with a searing edge of irony, "I wouldn't want to join any club that would accept me as a member."

Let it be known that brevity, not truth, is the soul

195

ABOVE. The Jefferson Room at the Farmington Country Club, Charlottesville, Virginia. The room was designed in 1803 by Thomas Jefferson for a plantation house. LEFT, TOP. The country club debutante. Drawing by William Hamilton. LEFT, BOTTOM. Ready to receive serve. Drawing by William Hamilton.

of wit. Not even Groucho could resist the fetching smile of country club life. In Los Angeles he was a member of the Hillcrest Country Club and in Palm Springs, the Tamarisk Country Club.

For those who seek such prizes, the country club can bestow on a family certain gifts of the golden rhythms of life. Across the landscape of America, on terraces shaded by green-and-white striped awnings or ancient oak trees, couples sip gin and tonics in the soft summer air. In the evening they will glide across the dance floor together. The following morning their children, with hair the color of candlelight, will play with other children at the pool. Men and women will play golf or tennis together or separately, and form friendships that will enrich the quality of their lives.

While clubs provide a spirit of continuity from generation to generation of families, they have also been witness to some rather fabled social and business (then, not now) incidents. As early as 1886 at the Tuxedo Club in Tuxedo Park, New York, at the club's first formal autumn ball, Griswold Lorillard, son of the founder, Pierre Lorillard, appeared in a tailless dress coat which today is named after the club and called a tuxedo.

At the 19th hole at the St. Andrew's Golf Club in Yonkers, New York, Charles Schwab put together the U.S. Steel Corporation by persuading member Andrew Carnegie to sell out to J.P. Morgan.

At the Chevy Chase Club in Chevy Chase, Maryland, member President Woodrow Wilson met and courted another member, Edith Bolling Galt. A few years later Wilson was on the golf course when he heard of the German sinking of the *Lusitania*. In September 1937 an accident happened at the Piping Rock Club in Locust Valley, New York, which not only has added to the club's lore but also to show business lore. Cole Porter, the great lyricist and composer, had just returned from Paris where his wife had announced her intention to divorce him. Porter was visiting Countess Edith de Zoppola in Oyster Bay and organized a riding party over the club's grounds. All was going well until Porter's horse, frightened by a strange noise, bucked, throwing Porter off. The horse stumbled and landed on Porter's legs. "When this horse fell on me," wrote Porter, "I was too

stunned to be conscious of the great pain. But until help came I worked on my lyrics for my song called 'At Long Last Love.'"

And it was at a Christmas dance in 1946 at the Apawamis Club in Rye, New York, that a young Navy pilot, Lieutenant George Herbert Walker Bush, was introduced to a girl named Barbara Pierce.

While country clubs rarely are known for being ahead of their time, occasionally history proves that they can be. In 1968 at the Baltusrol Golf Club in Springfield, New Jersey, member Richard M. Nixon held a meeting of prominent Republican leaders to discuss his upcoming presidential campaign; the press discovered Nixon was a member of a restricted club when they asked the club president about the club's policy. He gave them a proper club president's response: "No comment, gentlemen." When they questioned Nixon he responded by saying, "I'll try to change the club's policy from within." Four months later he resigned his membership.

Presently there are 5500 member-owned country or golf clubs in the United States. The average membership is between 400 and 600. The average club's gross revenue in dues, initiation fees, food, and athletic charges is between $2 and $5 million.

The exclusiveness and upper-class status of country club life has served those in the advertising industry who wish to evoke a distinct life style for their products. Even around the turn of the century real estate developers with houses only remotely near country clubs advertised "the best in country club estate living." Sporting goods manufacturers promised sportsmen that they could play better with "country club model" golf clubs or tennis racquets. Clothing manufacturers have all but redressed men who wanted the country club look. One manufacturer in the 1920s advertised "the all cotton country club dress shirt." Even a shoe polish manufacturer promised men that if they bought his product they would have "a country club shine."

In the 1950s General Motors promoted its "Country Club station wagon" as the "latest luxury station wagon to drive." A food manufacturer seeking a more discriminating buyer came out with a "country club rye bread." Even Bermuda, in the 1980s, was extolling its beautiful beaches, golf courses, tennis courts, and friendly people by saying "come to our country club in the Atlantic."

On and on the advertisements go. Indeed, no other American social institution has been used to promise so much to so many who knew so little of the realities of country club life.

But what is a country club? It is best defined by saying what a country club is not. It's not democratic and never claimed to be. In fact, it's a revolt against and negation of democracy; it's a small group that sets itself apart from the majority, building a social wall around its pastimes. Even a club's president is not elected by members but is appointed by the board of governors.

A country club is not an alternative to the home and it's not even a home away from home where one can do, within the bylaws, as one pleases. That wasn't always the case, however. In 1929 a reporter for *Time* described one of the Myopia Hunt Club's members, one Frederick Prince, as "testy," "box-jawed," and "priest of all financial oldsters." It was an apt description of Prince at age seventy. In the summer of 1929 Prince got into a spirited game of polo and in the heat of battle threatened an opposing player, saying that if he didn't get out of the way he would kill him. When the man didn't, Prince was almost true to his word, splitting the man's head open with his mallet. Prince paid $15,000 in damages.

A fellow member, Quincy Adams Shaw II, having taken up the case of the injured man, insisted on having Prince expelled. However, it turned out that Prince—the last surviving brother of the Prince family, who founded the club—enjoyed a life membership at Myopia and was immune to such judgment. This was at a time when club bylaws overrode practically all social codes.

Less than ten years later, clubs began taking strict action against certain members' recalcitrant behavior. A case in point is the Howard Hughes incident at Bel-Air Country Club in 1938.

At 11 o'clock on a Friday morning in early May the club's golf pro received a call from one of the club's wealthier members, Mr. Howard Hughes. He told the pro that, although he was then in Santa Barbara, he was definitely keeping his one o'clock golf date with member Miss Katharine Hepburn.

The pro thought little of the call until he realized that Santa Barbara was a good three hours' drive away. But, at five minutes to one, a single engine plane piloted by Hughes circled the golf course once and then made a smooth landing on the eighth fairway. Howard Hughes or not, the members were in an uproar and promptly called the sheriff's office, who had the plane grounded. There was an urgent meeting of the board of governors. Hughes was fined for such conduct unbecoming a Bel-Air member. Instead of paying the fine, Hughes simply resigned.

By the 1960s, clubs were increasingly intolerant not just with members who overstepped social niceties but also with members who headed committees. At an annual meeting at the Merion Golf Club in Ardmore, Pennsylvania, a member rose and demanded to know by whose authority a vine of honeysuckle had been removed from an out-of-bounds fence on the incoming nine. The chairman of the green committee replied that it had been done by his authority. An argument ensued and it was determined that the green chairman had overstepped his authority. He resigned from the committee then and there.

The idea for the first country club in the United States probably began as early as 1860, with seventy prominent men from Boston. Twenty-two years elapsed before the idea became a reality. While The Country Club was an original, the name wasn't. In the 1870s one of the founding members, James Murray Forbes, was working in the China trade and while in Shanghai, frequently visited a British club called The Country Club. As Dixon Wecter wrote in *The Saga of American Society*, "The Country Club has never assumed a place name because it is *sui generis* like the roc's egg."

In April 1882, Forbes invited thirty-four friends to dinner (thirty-three of them were members of the Somerset Club) to discuss the official formation of a country club.

This news was quickly reported in the *Brookline Chronicle:* "It is proposed to organize a Country Club at Clyde Park, and a number of gentlemen prominent in the clubs and social circles of Boston have issued a circular explaining the aims and objectives of the club. The general idea is to have a comfortable clubhouse for the

197

use of members with their families, a simple restaurant, bedrooms, bowling alley, lawn tennis, a racing track, etc." Also, to have horse races occasionally and music in the afternoon. Then as now, a country club was defined as a family club of mutually congenial people organized for sporting and social gatherings.

Forbes concluded his prospectus for The Country Club: "True sport promoted and practiced by true sportsmen, true gentlemen and true friends."

If professional sports today seem more a festering of disagreements—players' versus owners' rights option clauses—than the wonderful preciseness of double plays and off-tackle runs, a century ago it was different. It was worse. Contest fixing was more the rule than the exception. Bribery was commonplace. Gamblers ruled professional sports. From 1880 to the turn of the century amateur associations sprang up, defining and codifying the rules for amateur athletes. In 1881 the United States Lawn Tennis Association (now the USTA) was organized. In 1888 the Amateur Athletic Union was formed. In 1893 the Jockey Club began. And in 1894 the United States Golf Association was formed. The National Steeplechase Association was formed in 1891, and in 1907 the United States Squash Racquets Association was formed. Supported and encouraged by the country clubs, the amateur organizations emphasized good sportsmanship and ethical conduct, and these qualities gradually had a beneficial effect on the professional sports as well.

Although The Country Club rightfully claims to be the father of country clubs, its contribution to sport in the United States is without equal by any other club. And its members have won more national championships than any other club. There was the "First Lady of U.S. Tennis," Hazel Hotchkiss Wightman, winner of forty-four national titles and donator of the Wightman Cup for women's tennis. Although she played most of her tennis at nearby Longwood Cricket Club, she maintained a regular membership at The Country Club. Although she played most of her tennis at nearby Longwood Tennis Club, she maintained a regular membership at The Country Club.

The first prominent female figure skater of the United States was club member Theresa Weld (Mrs.

Charles Blanchard). In 1914 she became the U.S. Ladies' Figure Skating Champion and again held the title from 1920 to 1924. She and club member Nathaniel Niles won the Paris doubles championships in the years 1918 to 1927 (except for 1919).

Two decades later the pond at The Country Club was the training ice for another young skater, Tenley Albright, who took up skating to strengthen her legs after being afflicted with polio. In costumes made by her grandmother, Miss Albright skated her way into national and international prominence. In 1951 she won the U.S. Girls Junior Championship and, from 1952 to 1956, was the U.S. Singles Female Champion. In 1952 she won a silver medal in the Olympics and in 1956 the gold. Then, following a family tradition, she entered Harvard medical school and became a surgeon.

In the northeast, other clubs began to sprout up. In 1884 the Country Club of Westchester County began. It developed from a suggestion to organize a tennis club into a club where all country sports could be enjoyed. The club boasted tennis courts, a polo field, a racetrack, a baseball diamond, traps for live pigeon shooting, boats, a bath house, and a pack of hounds.

Not to be outdone, two years later Pierre Lorillard III, scion of the snuff and tobacco fortune, created the most opulent club of all at Tuxedo Park, forty miles northeast of New York City. On 7000 acres of the 600,000 that he owned, Lorillard, in collaboration with the architect Bruce Price (the father of Emily Post) created twenty-two dormered cottages weathered to medieval charm, a huge wooden clubhouse, stables, a swimming tank, a trout hatchery, and a gatehouse that Price once described as looking "like the frontispiece of an English novel." Its initial cost was a whopping $1.5 million. Several years later he spent $2 million building a golf course, a racetrack, and a mile-long toboggan slide. The club, of course, was only for the very right people: William Waldorf Astor, C. Oliver Iselin, Ogden Mills, and Sir Roderick Cameron, the British Consul in New York.

Thus supported by the interest in equine sports and the love of sport, many country clubs of the 1880s flourished. But it took something else for them to spring up everywhere, establishing themselves as a social insti-

**ABOVE.** At The Country Club, Brookline, Massachusetts. The clubhouse is in the background. *(Left to right)* C. Mackay, Mrs. Gerald W. Blakeley, nee Tenley Albright, the champion figure skater, and the late Thomas B. Frost. **LEFT.** Jimmy Demaret *(right)* gives a golf lesson to Bel-Air Country Club member Bing Crosby in a scene from a film made for the National Caddy Foundation.

**ABOVE.** A view from Tuxedo Lake: the clubhouse of the Tuxedo Club, Tuxedo Park, New York. **RIGHT.** Sam Snead *(left)* accepts prize money from Bel-Air member Ray Bolger for winning the Joe Novak Pro-Am.

tution. What was needed was a sport for all ages, for men and women, that would attract, amuse, and add a new dimension to country club life.

In 1888, in Yonkers, New York, a transplanted Scotsman named John Reid founded the St. Andrew's Golf Club. Although there was some kind of golf played in the United States earlier than that, particularly in Charleston, South Carolina, as early as 1786 and in Savannah, Georgia, at the Savannah Golf Club, neither established the game itself. Reid's timing was impeccable. Golf answered members' needs and further served as a means of promoting and developing country club life. The game had been heralded by able Scottish writers and was recommended by statesmen. Thus, golf arrived in the United States with centuries of history behind it and a continent before it.

Alone, golf might have remained merely a game and the country club a rural spot for the upper classes. Together, they became a way of life.

In *The Story of American Golf* writer Herbert Warren Wind best described the appeal of golf: "Golf started off with a great advantage over many other sports: you did not have to be a young, fast, beautifully coordinated athlete to play it acceptably. As a result, it found ready converts among the two sexes and people of all ages. They soon discovered that once golf gets you in its grip, it never lets you go. On the one hand, there was Andrew Carnegie declaring thoughtfully that golf was 'an indispensable adjunct of high civilization' and on the other there was the story of the Scotsman who threw his clubs into the ocean after a bad round and nearly drowned trying to rescue them. Both statements added up to about the same thing."

Sociologist Mark Benny theorized that golf's extreme popularity with the American businessman was because it answered his needs as the independent capitalist. In the act of hitting a ball from hole to hole, the golfer symbolically is directing his destiny. In short, golf is a game of laissez faire. It is not coincidental, Benny stated, that both golf and Adam Smith came out of Scotland at the same time.

In 1893 golf arrived at The Country Club. Members Lawrence Curtis, Arthur Hunnewell, and Robert Bacon had a six-hole course built for $50. When the course was completed they gave an exhibition for the members, most of whom had never seen this new game. Hunnewell was the first to tee off. His tee shot on the first hole, a 90-yard par 3, was struck wonderfully. The ball landed on the edge of the green and rolled slowly into the cup, a hole-in-one. The only reaction his feat elicited from the gallery of staunch horsemen was a mild disappointment when he failed to duplicate his feat on the second hole. They thought Hunnewell's game was not all that it should be.

From the late 1880s, when there were fewer than a dozen golf and country clubs in the United States, this social institution blossomed. By 1908 there were more than a thousand. Some of the first were The Apawamis Club (1890), the Philadelphia Country Club (1890), Shinnecock Hills Golf Club (1891), Maidstone Club (1891), Palmetto Golf Club (1892), Chevy Chase Club (1893), Newport Golf Club (1893), Onwentsia Country Club (1895), Country Club of Detroit (1897), the Los Angeles Country Club (1897), Oakmont Country Club (1903), and the Country Club of Virginia (1908).

In 1895 a gentleman farmer named Louis Keller, a small deaf man with sandy hair, a drooping mustache, and a high squeaky voice, formed the Baltusrol Golf Club in Springfield, New Jersey. Today, Louis Keller is but a footnote in the world of clubdom, but clubs have been indebted to him for over a century. He's better known as the founder of that black and red book, the *Social Register,* first published in 1887. Tactfully, Keller never included his own name. But golf and country clubs were included, and now number forty.

Golf's popularity even invaded the hunt clubs. On Boston's North Shore in Hamilton, the Myopia Hunt Club built a course in 1893 that was good enough to host three U.S. Opens. On Long Island's North Shore the Meadow Brook Club, the fountainhead of polo and fox hunting, put in a course in 1892 that was good enough to host the first U.S. Women's Amateur. Meadow Brook's arch polo rival on Long Island's South Shore, The Rockaway Hunting Club, built a course in 1892.

Country club life kept gaining in popularity as it was praised by a variety of people who were tireless in descriptions of its ethos. "The real all-year-around country club," one writer wrote, "so-called, is strictly speak-

**201**

ing suburban and owes its importance sociologically to that fact. It exists because the American who does business in a city, or lives there, has been seized with an uncontrollable and most commendable desire to be outdoors; and it promises to be a safety-valve of an overworked nation." How true! More remarkable, the statement appeared in *Outing Magazine* in June 1901. When Henry James returned to the United States after a thirty-year absence he thoughtfully declared that country clubs were a perfect place for the elite to relax.

And the elite did. While the golf courses began as the star—thanks to such brilliant golf course architects as Donald Ross and Charlie Blair Macdonald, followed by such gifted architects as A.J. Tillinghast and Alister Mackenzie—they slowly relinquished this role to the clubhouse. From the modestly handsome clubhouse designed by Stanford White at Shinnecock Hills, the clubhouses grew and grew. Outside of Chicago the members of the Medinah Country Club built a clubhouse half a city block long, with flooring of imported Italian marble. The club not only had a course for men only, but also a course for women only.

Soon clubhouses had indoor tennis courts, squash racquet courts, swimming pools, bowling alleys, bridge rooms, billiards rooms, and ballrooms. From the fairway the large clubhouses resembled unlaunched luxury ocean liners.

One of the most ambitious plans—not only for a clubhouse but also for a club—was the Westchester-Biltmore Country Club in Harrison, New York. (It is now the Westchester Country Club and site of an annual PGA Tour tournament.) The club was the dream of John McEntee Bowman, who in 1919 was president of the Bowman-Biltmore Hotel chain, one of the largest chains of hostelries in the world.

Bowman envisioned a club for millionaire sportsmen. It would have a year-round resort hotel. Members would either live in the hotel or in homes around the grounds of almost 624 acres. A huge staff of chefs, cooks, and waiters would take care of all meals in the hotels and in the homes. There would be maids and gardeners. A platoon of mechanics would take care of the members' cars. There might even be an airfield. The sporting facilities would include two golf courses de-

signed by Walter Travis, grass tennis courts, polo, horseback riding, swimming, boating, a squash racquet course, tobogganing, skating, shooting, and even skiing. The club was to open in 1920 and the initial cost was estimated at $2 million. The club finally opened on May 25, 1922, and the total cost exceeded $6 million, although not all the grandiose plans were realized. Fifteen hundred members joined the club and paid an initiation fee of $25.

The club experienced seven lavish years of existence. Meanwhile, Bowman had built other hotels—the Seville Biltmore in Havana, the Los Angeles Biltmore, the Providence Biltmore, and the Miami Biltmore in Coral Gables. Finally in the spring of 1929 Bowman merged his properties, including the club, into the United Hotels Corporation. One of the main reasons was that his club's operating expenses showed a net loss of over $5 million. The members finally purchased the club.

While it seemed all this time that country clubs were the private realm of people of Anglo-Saxon Protestant heritage, excluding Irish Catholics and Jews, they weren't. Affluent Irish Catholics were among the founding families of the summer colony of Southampton and Shinnecock Hills Golf Club and National Golf Links of America. The Winged Foot Golf Club drew a large proportion of its membership from the New York Athletic Club, which had a large Irish Catholic membership.

One of the first Jewish country clubs was the Century Country Club in Purchase, New York, founded in 1898, and its membership was predominantly German Jews of Wall Street. Another early club was the Losantiville Country Club in Cincinnati, Ohio, founded in 1907. It's not coincidental that Cincinnati would have one of the earliest and most prestigious country clubs. Cincinnati's Jewish population dates back to the mid-nineteenth century, and its Hebrew Union College Jewish Theological School is the oldest rabbinical seminary in the Americas, founded in 1875.

The eastern Jewish clubs practiced their own subtle form of exclusion, often by not taking in "Orientals," which was a gentle euphemistic term for eastern European Jews. As recently as a fifteen years ago a potential member of Quaker Ridge Golf Club, which has

**ABOVE.** The sprawling clubhouse of the Westchester Country Club, which opened in 1922 at a cost of over $6 million. **LEFT.** The elegant clubhouse of the River Oaks Country Club in Houston, Texas.

**ABOVE, TOP.** Carriage Day at the Newport Country Club, Newport, Rhode Island. **ABOVE.** Golf, country club style. Drawing by Arnold Roth.

one of the best golf courses in the country, had to submit the name of his maternal grandmother.

No such problem existed in Los Angeles. With a burgeoning population of eastern European Jews in the motion picture industry—producers, directors, actors—there was need for a club; Hillcrest Country Club opened in 1920. If there ever was a country club in the country guaranteed to make people laugh, it was Hillcrest. Into the mid-1970s a regular round table for lunch consisted of George Burns, Groucho Marx, Jack Benny, and Milton Berle.

It's a common belief that Hillcrest was formed because the Los Angeles Country Club wouldn't take in any Jewish entertainers. The fact is, the LA Country Club doesn't take in anyone, Jew or Gentile, in the entertainment business. Actor Robert Stack, who was from one of Los Angeles's oldest families and who grew up playing polo and golf, had to resign from LA Country Club when he became an actor. Whereupon he joined the happy mix of show business and non-show business members at Bel-Air Country Club. One actor wanted desperately to get into the LA Country Club and went so far as to send its board of governors critics' unfavorable reviews of his work to prove he wasn't an actor.

Quite by accident one actor did slip into membership at LA Country Club: Randolph Scott. By that time he had stopped starring in motion pictures, was in the oil business, and had a house adjacent to the club's 5th green on the North Course. He had gotten in because he applied for membership under his real name of George Randolph Crane. The club's officers made the best of it and in their own way tried to resolve the matter. One evening, after Scott and his wife were leaving after dinner, a member of the club's board of governors approached him and said, "Mr. Scott, the club's board of governors would greatly appreciate it if you could do your best to keep your old movies off television."

Indeed, when it comes to botching a situation and actually compounding the problem, no one does it better than country club members. At the Philadelphia Country Club in the late 1930s member Mrs. Edwin Vare (the great Glenna Collett, winner of six Women's Amateur championships) decided for the one and only time to play in the club's ladies championship. The golf

committee had ordered a silver cup from Philadelphia's famed jewelry store Bailey, Banks and Biddle. By the time Mrs. Vare had reached the 7th hole she was several shots ahead of her opponents and unlikely to falter. But the cup had not yet arrived from Bailey, Banks and Biddle. A call was put through to the store, and its manager assured the chairman of the golf committee that the cup was on the way. A half hour passed and still no cup. By the time Mrs. Vare reached the 14th hole and was way out in front, the cup still hadn't arrived. The chairman told a member of the board of governors that he would go home, get a cup one of his dogs had won, polish it up, give it to Mrs. Vare, and explain later. It seemed like a good idea. The cup was placed on a white tablecloth on a table just off the 18th green. After Mrs. Vare holed her final putt for victory, there was a brief ceremony, and she was presented with the cup. She looked at it, then put it on the table and walked away in a huff. The bewildered head of the golf committee picked up the cup and finally read the inscription: "For the best bitch in show."

The depression of the 1930s took an enormous toll on clubs. At least one fifth of the clubs went under. The attrition rate would have been higher had it not been for some enormously wealthy members who personally went so far as to supplement their clubs' payrolls. Services were cut and many clubs contracted by selling off land. Membership dues were reduced and in many cases, to get new members, initiation fees were waived. Then, just as the Great Depression seemed to be ending and clubs were getting back on their feet, World War II began. Fairways were turned into victory gardens and those clubs in rural areas often let cattle graze on their fairways. Maintenance of the golf courses and tennis courts was highly reduced because of gasoline rationing and the difficulty of getting new parts for machines. Those clubs near armed forces facilities took in officers as new members at a nominal fee. And whenever possible, the clubs did their part when organizations such as the Red Cross called upon them to host golf or tennis exhibitions to raise money for them. When either an employee or a member was killed in action it was like a death in the family, and the club would fly the American flag at half mast.

With the end of World War II clubs tried to get back to normal as soon as possible. But it was a slow process. Even so, the United States Golf Association resumed its competitions as quickly as 1946, as did the Masters. Club membership began to climb. And as it had been before the war it was the captains of industry along with some entertainers who were the real joiners. J.P. Morgan once belonged to nineteen clubs, Cornelius Vanderbilt to fifteen, Averell Harriman to fourteen. Gus "Lightfoot" Walker, once president of First National City Bank, belonged to a staggering twenty-two clubs. In the entertainment field, Bing Crosby led the list with membership in some nineteen clubs.

By the mid-1950s country clubs were facing another problem: age. Those members who had guided clubs through the Great Depression and World War II were getting on in age. While in the past junior memberships were reserved only for members' children, now the sons and daughters had moved away. At the Apawamis Club in Rye, New York, junior memberships were open to non-members up to the age of thirty-four at a reasonable fee. Some members claimed that Apawamis had gone from blue blood to red blood. Maybe so. But new junior members quickly discovered that much of the old family tradition and money prevailed. "It's almost impossible to get a golf match for a $10 nassau. $2 is the going rate."

On Long Island's South Shore a similar program was set at the Rockaway Hunting Club with its interdependent Lawrence Beach Club, where a junior guest would have complete use of both facilities for two years at a very nominal fee. The Apawamis and Rockaway programs were imitated by other clubs in the New York Metropolitan area.

Although it may have appeared that the social boundaries at country clubs were loosening, it was merely illusory. In 1955 the Rumson Country Club in Rumson, New Jersey, a club that dates back to 1908, hired a young assistant pro—an intelligent, affable and Rice-educated Texan named Dave Marr. (He would go on to win the 1965 PGA championship and become a prominent television commentator.) One Saturday during young Marr's first month at the club he joined three members for a round of golf. Afterward they retreated to the grill for a few beers and that venerable club culinary staple, a club sandwich. Certainly not a unique situation. But three days later Marr received a letter from the club's president stating that henceforth he was not to fraternize socially with the members; and furthermore, being one of the help, he was to take all his meals in the kitchen. At the end of the season Marr resigned.

In the 1960s, with the strengthening of the civil rights movement, country clubs and their members began keeping a lower profile than usual. Those members who had dealings with the media were advised not to mention their club affiliation. In 1970 Robert Townsend, who had been chairman of the board of Avis Car Rental and director of Dun and Bradstreet wrote the bestseller, *Up the Organization.* A cover story about him in *Time* accurately stated that Townsend was a member of Augusta National Golf Club. The day the article appeared Townsend received a call from Augusta's autocratic president, Clifford Roberts, who informed Townsend that he would accept his resignation immediately. In 1970 President Nixon promoted G. Harold Carswell's nomination as Associate Justice of the Supreme Court. The first inquiry was enough. It revealed that when Carswell was U.S. Attorney for the Tallahassee area he had been a charter member and director of a club that acquired a municipal golf course and turned it into a private course. One critic construed such an act as "an indication of segregationist sentiment." Carswell wasn't nominated.

President Jimmy Carter met with equal unyielding scrutiny. The Attorney General designate, Griffin B. Bell, was a member of two Atlanta Clubs, the Piedmont Driving Club and the Capital City Club. Neither had black members and only a few Jewish members. Bell initially announced that he would do something before going up to Washington. "Up there," he said, "I would be the Attorney General and would be the man who, in a sense, stood for equality before the law." At first he mentioned that he would become a non-active member, and then he said he would resign. He wasn't confirmed. The designated director of the Office of Management, Bert Lance, quickly resigned from the Piedmont Driving Club, the Capital City Club, and the Atlantic Athletic Club.

In 1978 William Webster, a Federal appeals judge of St. Louis, was nominated as Director of the Federal Bureau of Investigation. Again, it appeared that a men's club affiliation would cause his defeat. Webster was a member of the St. Louis Country Club, a metropolitan club called the Noonday Club, and a Mardi Gras society called the Mysterious Order of the Veiled Prophets.

First, a member of the Anti-Defamation League of B'nai B'rith urged him to resign from his clubs immediately. Then the chairman of a St. Louis group called ACTION claimed Webster had "a consistent history of practicing racism, sexism and elitism." Instead of taking the defensive, Webster made no apologies and took the offensive. In the Senate confirmation hearings he was questioned by Edward Kennedy about his club affiliation. Webster articulately responded, "My intention is to do what I have always done, that is, to monitor them, and if I conclude there is any active discrimination, to leave, or if I conclude they are in any way impeding or interfering with the effective performance of my role as Director of the FBI, to leave them." Webster was confirmed and later appointed Director of the Central Intelligence Agency.

In August 1990 what still is referred to as the Shoal Creek Incident reverberated through country clubs like a gigantic thunderclap.

It was discovered that the Shoal Creek Golf Club in Alabama, which was to host the PGA Championship, didn't have a single minority member. The Southern Christian Leadership Conference accused the club of racism and threatened to protest. Sponsors pulled their advertising. The club took in a black member and the championship was played. Then in a matter of months all the golf associations—the Professional Golfers Association of America, the Professional Golfers' Association Tour, the Ladies' Professional Golfers Association, and the United States Golf Association—stated similar policies: that those clubs hosting tournaments in which they had a financial interest couldn't discriminate because of sex, creed, or color. What went almost unnoticed—and that was what the clubs wanted—was that a small percentage of clubs in the Northeast, around the Chicago area, and in the upper South, clubs

that didn't even want tournaments, had in the last decade and a half quietly and discreetly taken in black members who had become part of the community. And they had taken them in for the same reason they took any member in—because they could afford the club and would make good members.

Gender equality is another issue facing country clubs. Minnesota recently passed a law stating that country clubs cannot discriminate against women if they expect any tax benefits. Indeed, clubs have come a long way from the day when they used to have entrances to the clubhouse marked "Men Only." Clubs traditionally have treated widows very magnanimously, giving them greatly reduced—sometimes by half—annual dues and usually reducing their annual food and beverage allowance. Clubs remain divided (except in Minnesota) as to whether to take women in as regular members or associate members. These clubs give women annual dues lower than the male members, but their dues are climbing comparable to the males'. A female who's an associate member only has to pay the dues and no initiation fee or bond; however, when a female member marries her new husband has to go through the process, as a new member, of being sponsored and co-sponsored for membership. He also gets to pay the initiation fee or bond, which in the East can be as low as $6000 or at California's Big Canyon Country Club in Newport Beach can run as high as $130,000. Saturday and Sunday morning tee times for "men only" are vanishing as women continue to mark progress in the daily work force. Female members also are being appointed to clubs' boards of governors. Clubs discreetly are staying out of the murky matter of divorce. Club membership, along with who gets the house and sports car, is a private matter.

Then there are taxes, the same problem that toppled the great estates—the genesis of the American country club. For many clubs, property taxes have increased one hundred percent in the last decade. Now sixty percent of a country club's revenue goes to pay the

207

OVERLEAF. At the Longwood Cricket Club outside Boston, club president Christine A. Creelman rallies with pro Bud Schulz. The chateaulike clubhouse is in the background.

taxes and maintenance cost of the golf course. One club in New York's Westchester County (which has more than sixty clubs) believed it had a unique solution to the tax problem. After the club's property tax exceeded $150,000, the club made the town's tax assessor a member. "Goddamn it," said the club manager, "the next year our taxes still went up. The assessor said if he didn't raise our taxes he would be showing favoritism." There was no mention of whether the assessor was asked to resign.

In certain major metropolitan areas around the country, where there's a premium on land— Philadelphia, New York, Boston, Chicago, San Francisco, Los Angeles—property taxes on clubs with an average of 160 acres could, if unchecked, accelerate to half a million by the end of the decade. Helping to hold back the high tide of taxes, paradoxically, are the clubs' golf courses—beautiful open spaces, privately maintained, enhancing and preserving communities and serving as a vast fresh air factory.

The desperate plight of one country club, in which property taxes threatened its existence, was resolved so resourcefully and creatively that it provided a song of hope for all country clubs.

The Richmond County Country Club on Staten Island, which in 1988 celebrated its centennial, remains the only country club in New York City. As of 1988 it was paying just over half a million in property tax, one of the highest in the nation. In 1989 New York City increased the club's assessment to $1.152 million. Rather than sell its golf course of 124 acres to a developer (the land was valued at $30 million) the club took the unique step of approaching the New York State Department of Environmental Conservation (DEC). In a landmark agreement the club decided to sell the golf course to the state for $4 million and lease it back from them for ninety-nine years, thus expanding parkland and ensuring the preservation of a greenbelt in a highly populated area. The deal also called for the club to give to the state four acres behind the 18th tee, land which adjoins the High Rock Park Nature Conservation Center, and then to create a 1000-square-foot scenic overlook behind the 10th hole. When the golf course became state parkland, it was taken off the city's tax roll.

Yes, the landscape of country club life is changing, but one of the constants, coursing through club history for more than a century, is the guardianship of club members' tribal mores and even morals. Not so long ago, on Long Island's North Shore, a club gave a dinner dance. During the evening two guests became romantically involved and although they were married, it wasn't to each other. They discreetly left the ballroom, seeking a place where they could be along to pursue their amorous adventure. They walked out on the golf course and accidentally stumbled into the sand trap by the 18th green. There were some pleasurable sighs and moans. A guard who protected the club grounds at night heard the sounds, walked to the edge of the sand trap, shone his flashlight on the couple, and properly asked, "Are you members?"

The embarrassed man, hoping the guard would leave, lied and said, "Yes, we are."

But the officious guard stood his ground and motioned with his flashlight for the couple to leave. They got up, walked out of the sand trap, and toward the clubhouse. The guard again shone his flashlight at the sand trap and the departing couple and said, "Stop! You can't be members. No member of this club would leave a sand trap unraked."

*"Even for the Los Angeles Country Club, that's a bit much."*

# Selected Bibliography

## Books

Aarons, Slim. *A Wonderful Time.* New York: Harper & Row, 1974.

Aldrich, Nelson, Jr. *Old Money.* New York: Alfred A. Knopf, 1988.

Amory, Cleveland. *The Proper Bostonians.* New York: E.P. Dutton, 1947.

_____. *Who Killed Society?* New York: Harper & Brothers, 1960.

Baltzell, Digby E. *The Protestant Establishment: Aristocracy and Caste in America.* New York: Random House, 1964.

Best, Hugh. *Thunderbird Country Club.* Palm Springs: 1986.

Birmingham, Stephen. *Our Crowd.* New York: Harper & Row, 1967.

Cappers, Elmer Osgood. *Centennial History of the Country Club.* Brookline, Massachusetts: 1981.

Chieger, Bob and Sullivan, Pat. *Inside Golf: Quotations on the Royal and Ancient Game.* New York: Atheneum, 1985.

Cornish, Geoffrey S. and Ronald E. Whitten. *The Golf Course.* New York: Rutledge Press, 1981.

Davis, William H. *The One Hundred Greatest Golf Courses And Then Some.* Norwalk, Connecticut: Golf Digest/Tennis, Inc., 1982.

Dobereiner, Peter. *The Glorious World of Golf.* New York: McGraw-Hill, 1973.

Glenn, Rhonda. *The Illustrated History of Women's Golf.* Dallas, Texas: Taylor, 1991.

Goodner, Ross. *The 75-Year History of Shinnecock Hills Golf Club.* Southampton: 1966.

Jenkins, Dan. *The Best 18 Golf Holes in America.* New York: Delacorte Press, 1966.

Jones, Robert Trent. *Golf's Magnificent Challenge.* New York: McGraw-Hill, 1988.

Miller, Dick. *Triumphant Journey.* New York: Holt, Rinehart and Winston, 1980.

Peper, George. *The First One Hundred Years of Golf in America.* New York: Harry Abrams, 1988.

Price, Charles. *The World of Golf.* New York: Random House, 1962.

Sommers, Robert. *The U.S. Open.* New York: Atheneum, 1987.

Steel, Donald and Ryde, Peter. *The Encyclopedia of Golf.* New York: The Viking Press, 1975.

Wechter, Dixon. *The Saga of American Society.* New York: Charles Scribner's Sons, 1937.

Wind, Herbert Warren. *The Story of American Golf.* New York: Alfred A. Knopf, 1975.

## Periodicals

*The American Golfer*

*Boston Globe*

*Golf Digest*

*Golf Journal*

*Golf*

*Golf World*

*New York*

*The New Yorker*

*The New York Times*

*Sports Illustrated*

*Staten Island Advocate*

*Time*

*Town & Country*

# Index

*(Boldface indicates photograph)*

213

215

## Photo Credits

i Patrick Ward **ii-iii** Paul Barton **iv** Paul Barton **vi** Paul Barton **viii** Tony Roberts **2** *Town & Country;* courtesy The Social Register **4** Edvin Levick/*Town & Country; Town & Country* **7** Arnold Roth **8** United States Golf Association **10** USGA; Dallas Public Library **14** Marvin Newman **16-17** Jerry Cooke **18** Courtesy Shinnecock Hills Golf Club **21** USGA **22** Suffolk County Historical Society; USGA **25** Robert Phillips; John Kelly **27** Brown Brothers; *Town & Country;* George Carroll Whipple III **28** Sky-Shots **30** Claudia Parks; Robert Phillips **32** Rameshwar Das **34** Mike Klemme/Golfoto **36** William Strode; Temple University **37-38** Tufts Archives **39** William Strode **40-41** Tufts Archives **43** William Strode **44-45** Tony Roberts **47** Brian Smith; courtesy Pine Needles Lodge and Country Club **48** Marvin Newman **51** Historical Society of Palm Beach County; Henry Morrison Flagler Museum; Historical Society of Palm Beach County **52** Historical Society of Palm Beach County **54** Marvin Newman; Slim Aarons; Dawn Coleman **57** Marvin Newman; Brian Smith **58-59** Patrick Ward **61** Courtesy Jupiter Hills Club **62** Tony Roberts **63** Red Morgan **64-65** Tony Roberts/courtesy Old Marsh Golf Club **66** Red Morgan **68** Tony Roberts **70** Arthur Hills/Bighorn **73** Courtesy Thunderbird Country Club **74-75** Tony Roberts **76** Courtesy PGA of America; Robert Phillips **77** Charles Saxon/*Town & Country* **78** Tony Roberts **80-81** David Ball/The Stock Market **83** Michael Salas/The Image Bank; Charles Saxon/*Town & Country;* Tony Roberts **84** John Kelly **86** The Image Bank **89** Marvin Newman; Rob Kinmonth **90** Courtesy Pebble Beach Company Archives; *Town & Country;* Courtesy Pebble Beach Company Archives **93** Slim Aarons/Rob Kinmonth **94** USGA; Focus On Sports **96-97** Tom Hollyman **98** Andrea Pistolesi/The Image Bank **101** Tom Hollyman; USGA **103** Marvin Newman/The Image Bank; Tony Roberts **104** Tony Roberts **106** Paul Barton **107** David Madison/Focus On Sports **108** Courtesy Bermuda Department of Tourism; Mike Klemme/Golfoto **109** Courtesy Kapalua Resort **110** Focus On Sports; AP/Wide World; *Town & Country* **111** Golfoto **112-113** Paul Barton **114** Courtesy Knollwood Country Club **115** Courtesy Siwanoy Country Club **116** Dost & Evans **117** Courtesy Winged Foot Golf Club **118** Sky-Shots; Rob Kinmonth **119** Courtesy Winged Foot Club **120** Courtesy St. Andrew's Golf Club **121** *Town & Country;* Courtesy The Apawamis Club **122** Paul Barton **124** Patrick Ward **125** Paul Barton **126** Paul Barton **127** Slim Aarons **128-129** Slim Aarons **130** Brian Morgan **131** Nicholas Foster/The Image Bank; Brian Morgan **132** Patrick Ward **133** Patrick Ward; Chuck Lawliss/The Image Bank; Patrick Ward **134** Bettmann Archive; Ian Joy **135** Courtesy Bel-Air Country Club **136** Slim Aarons **137** Slim Aarons **138** Claudia Parks **139** Slim Aarons **140** Paul Barton **141** Paul Barton **142** USGA **143** Brian Morgan **144-145** John Kelly **146** Golfoto **147** Tony Roberts **148** Patrick Ward; Dost & Evans **149** Brian Morgan/Golfoto **150** Marvin Newman **151** Bill Hickey/The Image Bank; Courtesy Palmetto Golf Club **152** Herb Lavert/Photo Researchers; Courtesy Binky Albright **153** Julian Graham; Courtesy Wade Hampton Golf Club **154-155** Slim Aarons **156-157** Ronald Searle/*Town & Country* **158** Jules Alexander **159** Jules Alexander **160-161** Golfoto **162** Golfoto **163** Dost & Evans; Paul Barton **164-165** Brian Morgan **166** John Lewis Stage/The Image Bank **167** John Lewis Stage/The Image Bank; Tony Roberts **168** Sky-Shots; *Town & Country* **169** Mark Jenkinson/*The Met Golfer* **170** John Lewis Stage/The Image Bank **171** Brian Morgan **172-173** Frank Magro **174** Brian Morgan; Dost & Evans **175** Robert Walker **176** Dost & Evans **177** Paul Barton **178** Patrick Ward **179** Arthur Weaver **180** Bettmann Archive **181** Giles Guittard/The Image Bank; Slim Aarons **182** Slim Aarons **183** Rick Dole; Courtesy Bay Hill Club **184** Robert Lyons; Alan Bolesta **185** Frank Magro **186** Courtesy of the Rockefeller Archive Center **187** Harry Benson **188** USGA **189** Dost & Evans **190** *Town & Country* **192** Paul Warchol **194** William Hamilton; Arnold Roth **195** Bill Kozma **199** Slim Aarons; courtesy Champions Golf Club **200** George Carroll Whipple III; courtesy Bel-Air Country Club **203** Bill Kozma **204** William Strode; Arnold Roth **208-209** Jan Staller **210** Charles Saxon